Clarity From Within the Ashes of the Midnight Hour

Written by Rashad Kennedy

Illustrated by Keya Kat

TABLE OF CONTENTS

ACT I:
PEOPLE FALL IN LUST EVERYDAY AND CALL IT LOVE
PAGES 7-34

TITLES	POEM #
No Filter	1
Miss Every Now and Then	2
The Enigma	3
Midnight Regrets	4
Moments Frozen in Time	5
With Your Clothes On, I Saw You Naked	6
We Fall Deeper	7
The Unknown	8
We Are Art	9
No Words, Just Actions	10
Hi	11
Don't Do Drugs, Do Mine	12
Indonesia	13
Love Is...	14
Who Are You?	15
You Are...	16
If Sex Sells	17
Urgent Matters of the Night	18
Draped in Your Love	19
D.R.U.G.S	20
I Can't Quit You	21
Stuck On You	22
Substance Abuse	23
My Beautiful Vice	24

ACT II:
CRACKS WITHIN THE PERFECT PICTURE
PAGES 35-71

Jay Gatsby's Fantasy	25
Not Again, Yes Again	26
Desire vs. Fear	27
Manifesting Regrets	28
Don't Do Drugs	29
A Dance Made For 2	30
Let the Dog Lie	31
Giving Into Self Sabotage	32
Risking It All Blissfully	33
The Inner Debate Over You	34
What's Left Unsaid	35
Too Late	36
A Slow Death	37
Where Did You Go	38
Her Recovery/Her Cycle	39
When I Fell	40
Sonnet 425	41
The Clichéd, Thorny, Black Rose	42
Lie to Me Please	43
The Deconstruction of a Heartbroken Millennial	44
Diary Entry Number 1	45
Diary Entry Number 2	46
Old Voicemails	47
False Fantasies till We Wake Up	48
My Private Pity Party	49
Running from You	50
Angela My Angel	51
To Still Be in Love	52
Out Of My Mind	53
The Driveby	54
My Room	55
Faceless Tattooed Tears	56
You're Here When You're Gone	57

ACT III:
SCARS FROM THE FIRE
PAGES 73-113

TITLES	POEM #
Generation Gap	58
9 Dead Inside the Church Walls	59
They Took My Cousin from Me	60
Does It Make a Sound?	61
Asphalt Graveyards	62
The Hopeless Dreamer	63
America the Beautiful	64
DNA Psyche	65
"Black Paranoia"	66
The Lost Sonnet Written On Black Paper	67
Dear Mr. Orange	68
Lives Matter	69
What You Crying For	70
Why God?	71
Similarities	72
I Saw Them Take It from Me	73
Poisonous	74
Poisoned Minds of the Concrete Jungle	75
I Ain't From It, I Am From It	76
Survivor's Remorse	77
If in Police Custody	78
Target Practice American	79
Frustrated and Scared	80
Thirsty People's Conversations	81
The Suffocation Complex	82
The City Is Burning: The People Are Dying	83
Massa Looks Scared	84
I've Cried My Last Tear	85
The Good Die Young	86
Post Traumatic Stress Disorder	87
The Transition	88
Will You Make It Home?	89
If I Get Shot Today	90
Grow Up	91
The Death of Innocence	92
Kids These Days	93
Change	94
Constantly Scared	95
The Cycle Continues	96
It's Hot as Hell	97
In My City	98
Ugly Questions	99
Red Rain Drops Fall Anyways	100

ACT IV:
FADING AWAY
PAGES 114-143

Planet Lost	101
Falling Silent to Deaf Ears	102
Intoxicated/Honest Thoughts	103
Going Through the Motions Numb	104
The Aftermath of the Tornado	105
Buried Alive in a World So Ugly	106
Living Inside the Fire	107
Broken	108
Spinning Out Of Control	109
Self-Destructive Vices	110
I Lost You a Long Time Ago	111
We Don't Talk Anymore	112
Crumbling Walls	113
What I Left Under the Rubble	114
Heart Attacks Along the Battle Field	115
Bare and Vulnerable	116
The Truth Hurts	117
I Don't Wanna Be Happy	118
The Life Force	119
My Heartbeat	120
I Can't Even Breathe	121
Diary Entry Number 3	122
A Dancer's Simile	123
Breaking Points	124
Today Is the Day	125
Dying	126
Empty Hour Glasses Pt. 1	127

Titles	Poem #
The Little Letter	128
I Saw It Happen	129
Empty Hour Glasses Pt. 2	130
The Brief, Ageless Flame	131
Save Me	132
A Flower Grew Here	133
Brand New	134

Chapter V: Hope Restored
PAGES 145-198

TITLES	POEM #
Moving On and On	135
The Meaning	136
Regrets	137
Pep Talk	138
I Found Worth in My Pigment: History Through My Eyes	139
So Painful, So Beautiful	140
I Hope this Shit Offends: The Real Nigga Manifesto	141
I'm Black	142
Hate	143
The Needed Conversation in this War	144
The Angel that Danced on the Clouds	145
Serenity	146
The Kept Diary Page	147
The Crumbled Up Diary Page Before the Start Over	148
The Sent Diary Page	149
Looking For What I Lost or Never Found	150
Staring From the Ledge of Forever	151
Sonnet 999888	152
I Got These Questions for Ya	153
What I Know	154
Laid Out on the Table	155
The Lover's Prayer	156
I Want this Forever	157
Preserved Euphoria	158
I'm Scared Too	159
The Nervous Love Note	160
Shouting From the Mountain Tops	161
Meds Numb the Pain	162
Perfect Kills and the Real Feeds	163
Laid Up	164
The Vibe	165
So Thankful	166
Apologies Love	167
Transparent for the First Time	168
Your Kiss	169
Ghetto Ass Love	170
A Ratchet Romantic	171
The Dream	172
The Switch Up	173
You	174
What I Wanna Do	175
Something I Wrote for You	176
What I Always Needed	177
I Just Wanna Love You	178
I Prayed to God About You	179

Act VI
PAGE 199

Untitled Spirit	180

Clarity From Within the Ashes of the Midnight Hour

NO FILTER #1

I just wanna write my name
Inside your walls...
When your back arches
And your breath calls

On them midnight urges
That lasts lifetimes.
From moments to millenniums
I just want more time.

More seconds.
More hours.

This is an urgent feeling
That my mental devours.
You know this.
You tease me.

Don't hurt me girl!
It ain't that easy.
You're the drug
A fiend would steal and sell televisions for.

You're the reason why
I love Prince's song, *Adore*.
I adore every single inch
That involves you.

Mind.
Body.
Spirit.

I fucking adore you!

You are passion
In the purest form.
Cemented love

That can't transform.

I had to get this off my mental,
I believe this honestly.
Flaws and everything else
In your anatomy
Was created with this divine purpose.
So heavenly.
Sculptors could spend decades-
Still couldn't make you more perfectly.

You're mobile art that people crave for.
The reason why people say things like...
Like... "Why don't we have this anymore?"

You're a throwback.

Anytime I lay you down
Or you throw that thing back.

I stare first.

Observe your grace,
Then do what lovers do.
A lifetime of passion
I'll give it all to you.

Unfiltered.
Uncut.

That HD clear view.

MISS EVERY NOW AND THEN #2

I ain't yours.
        You ain't mine.
Not an equal playing field
        On this land mine.
Trying to watch my steps
        Before it blows up in my face.
Trying to slow my roll
        Before I lose this race.
Follows all the rules
        But you damn sure fine.
It always hits me hard
        Like a punch line.
You feed my soul,
        Like a lunch line.
It's all gourmet,
        Don't mean it's healthy for me.
Right under you
        Is where I wanna be.
That smile's addictive
        Like my favorite song.
In constant rotation,
        Top 40 from dusk to dawn.
Simple things like your lips
        Really turn me on.
It's complicated.
        So complicated.
Is it really fair
        That we stay complacent?
No good for you,
        No good for me.
I always see you
        In my daydreams.
Do you think about touching me
        When you go to sleep?
Chest to chest.
        Heart to heart.
When awake,

            We press pause.
But when we sleep,
            We press start.
Seems to be the motivation
            For our fantasies.
We ruin it all
            With our flawed visions of reality,
                    Broken views
                            Of morality…

THE ENIGMA #3

Pain in her essence.
Her name represented love.
She engulfed me whole.

MIDNIGHT REGRETS #4

I'd prefer for your love to be eternal,
But I'll settle for a night.

I'd love for you to be a safety net,
But this pillow will be just fine.

Pretend comforts are okay,
I'll lay down in the lies.

Honestly I'm willing to believe anything,
As long as you say them with your eyes.

I'll tell my heart to be quiet,
Even though it begs and it tries.

I listen and contemplate-
I never oblige.

I fiend for the feeling
To relax in your presence.

I fiend for this feeling
Ecstasy in your essence.

The lovers' prayer,
Said over and over again.

To pretend you love me,
That's my hearts biggest sin.

MOMENTS FROZEN IN TIME #5

In times like these
I fall deeper.
I can't stop.
She can't either.

Moments arise
When you arrive.
Rare moments
That electrify

Your spirit
While your body feels the vibe.

There's an effect you have on me
While I'm on the edge
Of this bed
Waiting for what's next.

It's the anticipation.
The rush. The sex.

I take my time
Ain't no need to stress.

Another lesson learned
Upon your campus.

A beautiful creation
As I stroke your canvas.

When I was younger,
All I thought about was kissing your lips.
A discovery was made.
Now I know that your lotus flower exists.

Brings my mind
To deeper fascinations.
I wanna bring your body
To new heights. New sensations.
Whenever it is.
Wherever it could be.

I don't believe in love
I just believe in you and me.
A flawed statement within societal morality,
But personally, I think we provide the beauty.

WITH YOUR CLOTHES ON, I SAW YOU NAKED #6

With your clothes on
I saw you naked.

It wasn't blatant
But I had to take it.

You bared it all to me,
It was clear to see.

You let my ears,
Represent your diary.

You were scared,
So was I.

We thought to be that open
That meant that you died.

Not right away
But you know, eventually.

Instead,
You found nirvana's harmony.

I respect that,
Hope to represent that.

Last week, I saw you naked.
It was all so real to me, nobody could fake that.

It wasn't physically,
It was spiritually,
It was dear to me.
You were so beautiful.
I'll remind you religiously.

WE FALL DEEPER #7

Lost in it all.
We fall deeper.
Love so cleansing
Like a preacher.

She washes away all my sins.
Pure in desire and nature.
Fatal attraction
Is the almighty creature

To take a hold of me
And my soul.
Engulfed in this feeling,
I can't let go.

Why should I?
The feeling is appealing.
So addictive that I pray
This isn't a false sense of healing.

Love is fierce. Love is strong.
It's slavery, enslaving me.
The man in me falls weak

To my knees.
I know my body is moving
Yet my soul can't speak.
It's reaching out.

Demanding!

"If I'm falling, catch me.
If I'm lost, find me.
If I need strength, hold me."
Weirdly...
No words are spoken.
Yet she hears everything.

Every word. Every syllable.
The other half of me.

With every touch
We become whole.
Inching closer and closer
To find every secret love has ever told,

I suppose.

THE UNKNOWN #8

Good God!
You excite me.
My spirit,
My entity.
It's your body
In the nighttime.
Your heartbeat
When the sun shines.

Look, I don't know what we are,
I couldn't even find it in Webster.
I just know this has to be something real,
This energy makes me nervous as these thoughts fester.
We're both broken.
We share that in common.
We ran away just to stumble on what could be,
Even though we know Cupid can't solve the problem.

Yet there's a comfort in us,
Almost as if we have the solutions to solve em.
Definitions are tricky.
Love is hard.
So how do we even define that,
When we don't even know what we are?

WE ARE ART #9

We are art
          You and me.
When I kiss your frame
          It's like poetry.
Your walk is like a song
          That keeps singing to me.
Melodically captivating,
          Enticingly hypnotic.
Inching towards me with a pace
          That goes on and on…
Don't you dare stop it!
          I hope to be your destination,
Filled with days that feel like vacations.
          You're the interior decorator
And my heart needs renovations.
          Ain't trying to make no more reservations
To the heartbreak hotel.

Even if I wasn't allowed to sing it
          I would climb the highest pedestal and yell…
"This witch put a spell on me!"
          But you're more like Glinda the Good Witch from *The Wizard of Oz*.
You are a masterpiece,
          Continually leaving me in awe.
Should be hung up in the Smithsonian
          Or like the Metropolitan Museum of Art or something.
You make me happy like that Pharrell song
          No, not that one.
The one that goes… "Don't be frontin'."
          Cuz I can't with you.
You are my flaws and my truths.
          My conscience swirls
With thoughts of you.
          Probably no good for me
But I like it.

We are an instant made romantic novel.
        I can't wait to write it.
But if we were a play
        Would we be a tragedy?
Or more like a romance
        Mixed in with traces of comedy.
Now that's something I would love to see
        With you.
So much art in the world I would love to make
        With you.

NO WORDS, JUST ACTIONS #10

Times when we're on this bed,
Our souls intertwine
And levitate within the moments
That are you and I.
When our bodies don't yet touch…
But we're hand to hand, eye to eye…
Then I stare at you as you slowly start to blush.
Your eyes look down as if you are a bit timid.
I kiss your forehead to revive the feeling.
For even in fear, I'll always have you, I'm committed.
Times like these
Fall silent to the truth.
For my vision is blind to my rearview
Or even in my future cuz it's right now where I have you.
Hoping that the feeling is eternal
As the candlesticks burn slow.
Baby trust, "Everything is everything,"
We live by that Lauryn Hill quote.
We subtract clothes
And add actions that leave us chest to chest.
It's your hips right there
That my hands start to caress.
The midnight hour,
That's our chance
To express passion

In this romance
Under the influence of our body's rhythm.
"OH... MY... GOD..." followed by whispers of yes.
Your touch is my command
I'll do anything your body suggests.

HI #11

Ships pass through the emerald sky.
I can feel the energy of hearts starting to dance.
Enigmatic feelings race through my veins,
I guess that's what the philosophers considered romance.
My two eyes saw your third eye
Centuries ago,
So I hoped our first meeting
Wouldn't be our plateau.
Cloud smoke
Makes me feel closer to the creator.
The stars aligned tonight
To tell you to meet me at the equator.
Meet me in the middle of the world
Where Jericho's walls start to fall down
And let's start over
From the rubble on the ground.
Heartbeats are the main producers
Where they are the only things that create sound.
But what if platinum plaques
Were just objects that we framed?
What if fame really meant
That nobody cares to know your name?
What if I was the only one that saw you?
But not the physical as mirrors are rearranged
To only show the imperfect thoughts
That show you as deranged.
But I only saw you as perfectly imperfect,
We're all crazy.
I hid it for years inside me,
But to hide it now, I'm way too lazy.
I don't wanna think,

I wanna feel.
I don't wanna act,
I wanna live out something that's real.
I wanna be able to do
And not be judged.
I wanna slowly lick your inner thigh
And watch your back raise high and juuuuuuuuussttt...
I wanna be able to get off topic
And enjoy where we're going.
I wanna show my soul
And not die because it's showing.
I would love to bare my soul
But it may die because it's lonely.
But honestly, what if I were you
And you were me?
Would you still be in awe
Of everything you see?
Would I trust every single word I hear
Or take it with a grain of salt?
Words can feed souls
But your hunger will never halt.
I see souls float everyday
Wondering will they ever stop.
Wondering how stressed they would be
If their bubbles were to ever pop.
But then it gets weird,
They dance with like this... like Vigor.
Then shape shift
Into different figures,
Usually,
Whatever you want them to be.
But honestly,
I just want someone to let me be me.
Truths dipped in acid,
Smoke blows out
As thoughts harassed us.
Luudes repackage the pain
But at the end of the day
They still come out the same.
White lines blurred

And I'm scared
As emotions begin to merge.
But then I felt your skin touching mine,
Expressing every adjective and every verb.
You make me feel scared... excited... high.
You ignite every urge. You're the drug I prefer.

DON'T DO DRUGS, DO MINE #12

Don't do drugs
Unless you do em with me.
I wanna lay up under you
For an eternity.
The weed smoke
We inhale and breathe
Seems to lead us
Towards our destiny.
Hate being sober
And you know that.
Clarity in this flawed, absolute world
They can have that.
I'll settle for this parallel universe
Where nobody can shatter me.
Where we as opposites converse
And connect like AA batteries
To plot on world domination
While we're on this bed.
You deliver a sensation
To my heart,
A spark,
The direct deposit
That never misses its mark.
But could it all end
Like when the smoke clears
Or the pills are gone
Or the lines disappear
And the feeling is gone.
Will your feelings still be here

Or do we need to be intoxicated
To act like peers?
Drugged up
To make believe you're here.
Faded
To wipe away the tears.
Fears are too painful
And you scare the hell out of me
Because you are the question mark
Against my sanity.
Bullet wounds burn up
And destroy my vanity.
I'm that guy
Or at least I thought so,
Then she rubbed
Her nose
And blinked her eyes and stared deep
And captured my soul.
My eyes are playing tricks on me
And the devil allures.
Drugs hit sharply
But you lie and pretend that they're the cure.
So you just take one more hit,
Close your eyes and endure
And hope your eyes don't roll back
And your nose don't fall off.
These are the casualties of lust in the morning.
I place you on my tongue and lift off.
Pure addiction,
You're the trip I just can't get off
And wouldn't want to anyways...

INDONESIA #13

I wanna live in Indonesia.
Somewhere high in the clouds.
I wanna live in the escape of our love.
Somewhere, where, our feet don't touch the ground.
I wanna be what movies taught us to be,
That clichéd, classic love story personified.
Euphoria around you always,
And it's magnified.
Ecstasy
In your lips.
Cocaine
In your hips.
Everything feels sped up
But I want it to slow down.
I can hear your heartbeat,
From up in the clouds.
Up here in Indonesia
I can only feel my heart and not my face.
Paranoia sets
Whenever I'm in this space.
I've been happy and in love lately,
Is this even real?
Or is this just the false nature in the land of Indonesia,
Where smoke clouds cloud your judgment and everything stands still.
Just to block your vision and your judgment
So you don't know what to give.
But this high has my soul lifted
And my mind stuck on what love really is.

LOVE IS... #14

I need Love.
I breathe Love.
I fiend for Love.

I dream Love.
Been team Love
Since a teen Love.

I found Love.
Then put down Love
While we make Love.

Dated for Love.
Hated Love.
Then ran away
Just to find shade from Love.

Ignored Love.
Adored Love.
Felt like an eternity
For the boy in me
To ride on the journey of Love.

You are Love.
I am Love.
We survive
Then get high off Love.

We fly
Into the night sky
For that
You and I Love.

We ramble for Love,
Gamble for Love,
Just to entangle ourselves
Within the intangibles of Love.

Happy, mad, sad,
Can't stand yo ass!" type Love.
That Screaming, "F you!" type Love
Then whispering softly
I wanna, "F you" type Love.

That Whenever Love...
Wherever Love...
Whatever Love...
While listening to
Maxwell Love.

That keep me calm through the storm
Type Love.
Or that I will cry for
Or die for
You type Love.

We can imagine
It all happens for Love.
Just means we may not want
But we do need Love.
For my soul screams, dreams and sings of Love.
Love... it even bleeds Love!
Can't you see it dripping off the sleeves love!?!?

WHO ARE YOU? #15

WHO...
Are you to love me
When I don't even...
Love myself?

WHO...
Are you to hold me
When I don't even...
Deserve your help?

WHO...
Are you to tease me
When I don't even
Have nothing left?

WHO...
Are you to love me
When I don't even...
Love myself?

YOU...
Are the Sun,
The Moon,
The Earth,
The Stars,
The whole entire solar system combined.

You...
Are the voice in my head,
The twinkle in my eyes
That make me wanna survive.

You...
Have sex appeal,
Are a full course meal,
With a contagious,
Life saving vibe.

So WHO...
Are you to feed me...
When outside in the cold
I was left?

WHO...
Are you to excite me
When my soul...
It was left for dead?

And WHO...
Are you to touch me
When I ignored
Everything I felt!?!?

Yes, WHO...
Are you to love me...
When I don't even...
Love myself ...?

YOU ARE... #16

Baby you're a blessing...
I see God in your essence...

Not to be around you is depressing...
I need your star in my presence...

To be without you is the end of the world,
That's the start of Armageddon.

Maybe then it can all start anew.
Even if the world ends today

I'll need this exact point of view.
The one that involves the sight of you.

You're like coffee on a fresh new day.
You're the front line for some fresh new Jays.

You're like freshly baked cookies on a hot new tray.
You're the hug that tells me everything will be ok.

You're happiness in the human form.
The living entity that I adore.

Good vibes is your uniform.
And I'm addicted ever so,

More and more.
You incite a hunger

Deep inside of me-
It feels so warm

It excites me.
You ask me,

"What's that one thing that makes me smile?"

I say "Baby you are...

Especially if you were next to me down the aisle...
Now that right there-

A happiness that would never go out of style.
In fact, let's just get married,

That would be wild."

IF SEX SELLS #17

If sex sells
We're going platinum.
A fortune 500 company
Couldn't replace this magic.

If sex sells
We're going platinum.
Diamonds with rubies of red,
Silk, furs, and dresses of satin.

I mean if sex sells
We're going platinum.
As we travel this plateau
And execute what our minds can fathom.

Baby, if sex sells
We're going platinum.
With the rhythm of this ocean
We are just mere waves cruising and crashing.

Ooo girl... if... sex... sells...
We have to go platinum!
People all over the world search for love,
But not all can experience this passion.

Because once sex sells

And actually goes platinum...
People don't buy records anymore
So it's a rarity when it happens.

So when our sex sells
And we do go platinum,
We won't even be able to speak
As our bodies are deep within this electric spasm.

Baby if sex sells
We're going platinum.
I love every move you make
You electrify me through your actions.

Love, if sex sells
We're going platinum.
Our playground has no boundaries
It is all we can imagine.

If sex sells
We're going platinum.
But it's priceless...
Every moment is priceless...

URGENT MATTERS OF THE NIGHT #18

I guarantee you know what we came to do.
So let me treat your body like you ain't been used to.
It's always the magic hour when it's just us two.
I need you right now, you're my bad influence.
Sweetest addiction. What my soul is missing.
We can make love on the floor of this kitchen.
Baby I just wanna lick you till your soul is missing.
Make sure we take our time and explore every position.
To electrify your senses is the only mission.
Our love deserves deeper compositions.
But I'm the helpless fiend whose skin is itching-
I crave the taste of you. It's strawberries cuz of your lotion,
By the way, became my favorite fruit.

DRAPED IN YOUR LOVE #19

Draped in your love
I don't need more regrets.
I just wanna be touched by the one,
I don't wanna regress.

I searched the earth and my feet are tired
So it's in your bed I slept.
My mind ran all day-
It was only here it could rest.
I need time.
I need love.
I need power.
I need us.

To be a now.
A forever thing.

Not something that just was...

D.R.U.G.S #20

You are addiction.
        No rehab just religion.
                I cannot quit you.

I CAN'T QUIT YOU #21

Honestly,
I just wanna feel your energy.
It's the heat of your body when you're up under me,
That makes it hard for me to wanna leave.

I'm the helpless fiend

Through you I live out every lust filled dream.
It was made with this magic,
A passion filled trance.
A dance of lust made for two

With occasional romance.

Trust me... I can feel the poison taking its toll.
Trust me... I know Cupid's evil twin brother shot my soul.
We ignore what's right for us
If we can convince ourselves that it's love.

So I remain vulnerable as I remove these gloves.

I lost this tug of war for my heart during the beginning stage.
I lust for you while in love with you, my heart is estranged.
I can't quit you and I wouldn't anyways.

STUCK ON YOU #22

Your kiss. My love. The drugs...
Play over and over again
Like a bell that just rung.
I can feel the vibrations
Of your spiritual energy
Enticing me. Internally.
It took control.

SUBSTANCE ABUSE #23

I need your touch to make me forget my flaws.
I need your voice to represent the love that never calls.

I'm trapped.
Lost in this space, somewhere out in the Netherlands.

Too bad I still got reception then,
So I press them messages that should never send.

What if they all got lost in the wires of them telephone poles,
Or those satellites up there that rarely seem to work... just float?

Then would you know that I'm addicted to you?
When I'm drunk or sober my thoughts still engross you?

That's the true definition of substance abuse.
The substance that hurts when I'm close or far from you.

Yet at the same time, peaceful whenever we're near each other.
I don't mean when we're here yet distant.

No I mean when we crave each other.
Right here right now, not sex but it feels like it.

Not poetry but it makes me wanna write it.
Not really a thing but ideas of the abstract.

Couldn't be in a play because these emotions, no one can act.
It was always real on my behalf

Even if you don't react the way I need you to.
When we're silent but my eyes are lost inside you.
Screaming,
Whispering,
      I
    Need
    You.

MY BEAUTIFUL VICE #24

She was candy coated cocaine in a wine glass
Dangerously
Served to me on a silver platter.
She was addictive,
Sweet and classy in my eyes.
She would lead to my demise.
I knew it and it didn't matter.
I ran away from her and instead ran into her arms.
A comfort I just couldn't afford.
Heartbreak could be my reward-
Pain I do adore.
Love in her voice.
With a trance deep within her eyes.
I stared and I stared and I stared...
Falling deep from within until I became fully hypnotized.
I'm in love with beautiful vices.
She shined brightest in the moonlight.
Candy coated curves.
Cocaine skin.
 Pure sexiness served in a wine glass.
You're the drug I crave for as I take my hit and take flight.
Whether good, bad, or indifferent-
This is where I lay my head at night.
Trust me when I say...
She was candy coated cocaine in a wine glass.

JAY GATSBY'S FANTASY #25

You are my green light across the dock by the bay.
A red beam violently flashes to destroy my vision.

Alarm blasting sirens attached to lions, tigers and bears
Couldn't stop me from craving you.

You are my American dream.
80s love story.
And adolescent fantasies.

Until I wake up
To a flawed reality.

Trapped within a nightmare,
I'll allow lust to paint my vivid fantasy of you

Into this life like vision
Completely.

NOT AGAIN, YES AGAIN #26

Entangled in love's grip.

Time escapes my grasp.

Weakened by emotions
I'm too frail to ask.

Dying slowly.

From my future, present, past
And any other scenario

Where I fear I had my last…

Breathe.

Feeling closer and closer
To this thing called love.

Instead I just see
The crying of doves.

I over indulge.

Until I overdose.

*Just gambling till I become
Comatose.*

I constantly lie to myself.

Then my heart rips out.

There's only so much you can *put it through*
Before your heart gives out.

Reduplicated as another mantle
Upon another shelf.

It's big game on the wall
That you hung up for yourself.

Yet my eyes stare
From the waves of her hair

To the road map curves
On a road less traveled I dared.

To run after a dream into the sun
For a moment in time,
To sacrifice my sanity

For what may not be mine.
Love is a gamble,
I just hope I don't crap out this time.

I lose myself in the fall before the crash
But I have time to parish.

It's all fun and games
Till you look towards marriage.

Mirages of lust.

Every moment I cherish.
Until I stop, look,
And listen.

My soul is still searching.
My heart comes up missing.

I should have been married by now-
We're both scared of commitment.

We should have been married by now-
Maybe we didn't pay attention.

Why weren't we married by now?

It started out as fun but never changed to make a difference!

Regrets Linger.

Tears stain.

I sit here amongst the chaos
Hoping these heart attacks weren't in vain.

The late nights all alone
With glasses tilted, Spirits spilled.
Love is a game made for two.

How can I play when I'm slowly losing my will?

I tell myself,
"No, not again."

But I know myself,
So yes, again.

DESIRE VS. FEAR #27

I've always wanted to fall in love
Quickly, I'll sabotage it.

I'm always running towards it.
Always running from it.

I don't know what I'm afraid of.
I just know I want it!

Regardless if I deserve it...

MANIFESTING REGRETS #28

We're no good,
But it feels good.

Opposites attract
When we don't know how to act.
Sticks and stones don't have the same impact
As those piercing words you use
To break me down or accuse.

I walk in this building and prepare for war.

Even if I don't know what I'm fighting for.
Lovers shouldn't equal fighters.
Running from truths like climate deniers-
It's getting too hot in this house.

Imagine if you were my spouse...

DON'T DO DRUGS #29

Baby you're so seductive.
Baby you're so destructive.
You could mend any broken heart if fate would have it.
But your anger could burn down any city if fate would let it.
She's a passionate,
Alluring,
Dangerous beauty.
The fire on top the stove where kids are drawn to be.
I'm the little kid walking towards pain that I'm excited to receive.
I don't know what it is about you.
We fight too damn much,
You know it's true.
When we make love
I feel this energy that can only be made between us two.
You're draining me.
This love is killing me.

A DANCE MADE FOR 2 #30

I see the arch of her back
Tempting me.
Saying,
"Look.
Stare.
Caress.
If you please."
Her eyes
Doing the devils dance
Of lust in the morning.

Honestly it felt like there was...
But there was no fair warning.
With lips so full like a selfish child's hands
In the cookie jar.

Our pure humanly needs inspire
An instant rush to the car.
Stars in my eyes,
Sin in my thoughts.
Helpless to it all.
A pure sexual intensity,
That's all she brought.

Simple things.

Like with the way her hips
Swayed, so tempting,
As her body dips
With the purest forms of lust
Of sweats and scents.
I'd be lying
If I said it all made sense.

Constant thoughts of what she wants with me.
My mind whispers...
  "Ecstasy."

She then concurs
With the whispers
Of sensual fantasies
Involving her and me.

An hour.
Simply,
Just an hour.
Oh how that sweet hour turns into three.

In my home
Where I reside
All alone,
Except for tonight.

"This night
That belongs to us."

A simple phrase
That was coined by us.
Out of sex, out of passion
Or purely out of lust.

It was communicated
As our bodies speak.
I close my eyes
As my soul becomes weak.

I swim calm
Into your troubled waters
Like I belong here.

So I'm never weary, I never falter.
I see your body call my name
Trapped inside your walls.

But oh!
Damn!
Baby!
You don't have to call.

LET THE DOG LIE #31

Lust on my mind.
Love in my heart.
Revel in the bad decisions,
Living off sparks.
Sparks of the blunt.
Sparks of the night.
We living what's wrong
But made it feel right.
There's a comfort in her eyes.
There's a safe haven in our lies.

GIVING IN TO SELF SABOTAGE #32

Heard this from poets in the 90s,
Cash rules everything around me.

So this what Imma do-
Imma let this cash reign up on your body.

Then Imma allow seduction to win
And temptation to rot

My moral compass
With everything you got.

Self sabotage
In the greatest form.

Lust keeps me high
While your body keeps me warm.

Are you the one I am supposed to be in bed with?
No.

We both knew this fact and we both said,
"So."

Why even think,
When we could react in the act of passion?

Are you the waves
That my boat is supposed to crash in?

I know you're not
But I treat you like the star destination that you are anyways.

Love is strong
But lust knows I'm its slave.

RISKING IT ALL BLISSFULLY #33

Wearing those pants that looked like they were painted on.
She did nothing wrong.
She just knew those certain actions to turn me on
And steer me wrong.
A path that was frequently chosen
For them girls with the bronzed skin that in the right light looked golden.

Especially when she was naked in the moonlight.
She rather just lay around the house naked than go out at night.
She rather be naked than hide her nature and that drew me in.
I hide all the time and wouldn't know where to begin,
I'm flawed...She crawled...
Towards me, engulfing me slowly.
While she inched towards vanity,
I lost my sanity. I blissfully gave it up
For a moment of euphoria entangled in lust.

THE INNER DEBATE OVER YOU #34

I need you.
    I shouldn't want you.
I love you.
    I can't receive you.
I lust for you.
    I can't believe you.
I fiend for you.
    You're the type of decision that haunts you.
I miss you.
    I can't think of you.
I dream about you
    I have interrupting nightmares about...
I want you
    But I surely can't need you...
  I think I want you
  Because I need you.

WHAT'S LEFT UNSAID #35

I've been more distant lately
I'm sorry.

Been on a worthless
Safari.

Trying to find them feelings I don't like,
But had-
Fuck it
I mean have.

Half of it
Wasn't that bad.

I mean we are happy,
But then we're sad,
All at the same time.

"I'm fine" really doesn't have the same meaning.
It's just a phrase replaced
For a spiritual healing.

A spiritual cleansing if we
Decease with all the lies.

It's teen spirit
The way you make me wanna hide
Rather than hear it.

It's more like the naked truth.
With all these thoughts,
I'm thinking of you.

Like a Frank Ocean song.
He was hiding to.
So am I wrong?

I can't admit the truth with everything to lose.
I've been living scared and you know it.

Do these feelings make you grow
Or just die slow?

Love just decays from our plateau to a crescendo.
Wish my spirit could be rinsed.
Wish I was a man made of tin.
Wish we could start over again.

We're just forgotten sins
That are never really gone.
Just ignored, never really touched on.
The ghost of fear's past.
We just pretend that it been gone.

Sorry if I'm rushing.
I hate staying complacent.
My mind is racing.
Wishing our bodies were adjacent
To how our hearts really feel.

Our souls are congruent.
We ignore that
Like lazy students
In this crash course called love.

We act like we don't match
And the sadder part is
We act like there's nothing wrong with that.

We just continue to make silence sound louder!
Why is that?
We probably both know why
We just don't know how to react.

TOO LATE #36

You love that woman?
Then fight!
Don't tell yourself
You'll have other nights!
Or worst...
What else am I missing out on?
Wake up
And turn the lights on
Before it's over,
Before she's gone.
Too late...

A SLOW DEATH #37

Tears on the pillow case.
Nightmares seeping through the sheets.
She don't wanna be alone
But barely wants to be with me.
I broke her like she broke me
But two wrongs don't make you right,
Just lost.

WHERE DID YOU GO #38

I asked my girl, "Where did you sleep last night?"
While in my arms,
She cheated, I knew it.
Not shocked or alarmed.
Relationships just rot
From the inside out.
Death comes swift.
Dying feels drawn out.
Probably started about three months ago,
My paranoia sets.
I keep my emotions hidden.
Fear leaves them bare and undressed.
I apologize in my mind,
Over and over.

She cheated, but I feel guilty.
I never told her…
I cheated too.
Way before it was even an issue,
Then again maybe it was.

Maybe she knew
I broke our trust.

She stares and responded,
"My body's here but my heart's gone…"

She read me my last rights; sadly, I knew what was going on.

"I was with my love last night…"

Guess I'm the obligation.

She said, "You probably met him before."
I said, "Damn… was it Nathan?"
"No."
She responded.

I hear her,
But desponded,

My mental is fading.

Now I know,
"Was it Alex?!?!"

Before she said anything I could feel the body blows.

I see his crooked smile
In my nightmares always.
I see their sex too,
Right up in them hallways.
I see it so vivid
I see it always.

"Yes." she said

No hesitation in her voice.
I see the look in her eyes
Attempting not to destroy
Me.

Too late.
Halfway dead
Like I can see the pearly gates.
Bullets began piercing my soul.
Full of deceit.

Maybe I deserve it all
-Here's my receipt.

I did this like suicide.
It's killing me.

HER RECOVERY/HER CYCLE #39

Why you over there looking all sad?
Ex dude hurting your heart and now you're talking all mad.

But I came here to fall in love.
You got the feeling messed up.

Up at maybe 3 AM.
You texting me so you ain't worried bout him.

But I came here to fall in love.
You got the feeling messed up.

Booty calls, I ain't worried bout that.
Imma service your body with every single thing I have.

But I came here to fall in love.
You got the feeling messed up.

I'm not some little play thing.
I'm definitely not for all these games.

I came here to fall in love
And you got the feeling messed up.

You're still in love with the ex dude that got you talking all mad.
Cried for hours and those dried up tears still got you looking all sad.

She isn't here to fall in love.
She just needs something to ease the pain
Since the feeling got messed up.

WHEN I FELL #40

I told her don't let me fall.
Now I can't feel my legs.
I feel like there are simple things I need.
I shouldn't have to beg.
I told her not to let me fall.
Now I'm on the ground
Staring at the broken pieces of this relationship like,
"What do I do now?"

SONNET 425 #41

You are my biggest regret
And trust me I've lived through many.
You are still the implanted false steps
Forever engraved in my memory.
You are nails scratching a chalk board.
You are guns being shot in the dark.
I can still feel you pulling me towards
The edge, sniffing the blood like a shark.
I still see you the same way I did on the last day
That I did on the first.
A beautiful angel in every way,
Except now you're the angel of death with a hearse.
Bitterly I'll say I love you.
Happily I'll say I loved you.

THE CLICHÉD, THORNY, BLACK ROSE #42

A black rose with skin piercing thorns
Wouldn't hurt me as bad.
Nor would an archer with heat seeking arrows
Who would let them fly with all they had.
My heart is black due to the blood flow,

It stopped.

Fear in my heart like I got 30 bricks in the passenger seat
As I'm about to get pulled over by the cops.

I'm surely done for.
I'm tired of being at war.
I'm always losing.
Not knowing what I'm fighting for.
I miss you.
From the first view-
Or at least what you used to be.
Now I'm too bruised to want to continue.
I bled out completely.

I'm still standing.

Just going through the motions while I'm falling
Through the sky without any form of landing.

I'm out of love
But I fell for you once…

Star crossed lovers
That seemed to be the prey for the hunt
To the beast called time
Along with an animal called fidelity.
The first time we had sex,
I wouldn't say you belonged to me.
Probably never made love,

Just a couple of passionate nights and early mornings.

But I confused it for more,
And now I lay here...

With the same fate as that corny dude
That I made fun of over there
When we accidentally met
At your labor day party.
I was arrogant,
With laughs so hardy.
I felt like the King
That would say off with his head.
Then later that night
You would end up in my bed.
I never gave a damn
About the blood being shed.
The hapless cuckold
Dying from the thorny black rose.
A cliché
That I would surely overdose.

My heart was dying,
Now it's comatose.
I didn't just love you more,
I loved you most
In a relationship made for two.
I now realize I shouldn't boast.

Both belong to somebody
In the beginning
And now we are nobody's
In the ending.

All I have are the stories
That were created and now told.
Damn that stepped on, spiteful,
Clichéd, thorny, rose.
A toast to the one I love and hate the most.

LIE TO ME PLEASE #43

I need your lies.
Please just lie.

Say you love me.
Leave me hypnotized.
You say you ain't perfect
Well so ain't I.

I need your love
I need your lies.

The truth just hurts.
I can feel it burn.
What are feelings anyway?
They just come out as words.

I just need your love,
Please allow me to believe.

I just want your love,
Allow a man to dream.

Let me lay down in the lies.
Right next to you.
Even if the truth is
That I don't know you.
I mean I used to
But that was a year ago.
Now I feel the distance
As I watched it grow.

So I rather just lie.
Baby let me lie.

You don't have to tell me.
You don't even have to try.
Just don't feed me these facts

That are no good for me.
I still need you here
So I won't allow nor watch you leave.

These lies
Keep me alive.

So baby just lie to me.
Feed me the lie.
Or you can walk away,
With God and the rest of the universe as a witness.
I'll slowly die where I stand
While you watch from a distance.

Truths burn.
Lies mend.

Just lie to my face
Even if I already know but refuse to understand.

THE DECONSTRUCTION OF A HEARTBROKEN MILLENNIAL #44

I look out towards the window
And s p a c e out.
I talk to the sky and ask for grace
Within the drought.
I look out there
Thinking I need somebody to save me.
Honestly I be staring out there
Hoping you would hear me.
If not my words then at least my thoughts
But pleads f
        a
          l
            l
              off towards deaf ears.
I would f
        a
         l
          l
            to my knees and beg
To kill my pride and release my fears.
I reached out to you some weeks ago
But I didn't hear nothing back.
Meant to tell you I love you and I'm sorry.
I didn't type that.
She made sure to let me know
She read it though.
I stared at that word "read" next to the time...
I couldn't let it go.
Man I hate stupid ass iPhones
And women be mad petty.
That's why dudes get mad and call women bitches!
Because we emotional... and petty.
Lately, more and more,
I've been internet heavy.
Airing out all our problems on social networks.
Couldn't say it face to face.

Easier to send that subtweet
Than actually going to your place.
Hate is easy.
Love is hard.
That's why I lash out
Instead of trying to find out where you are.
Searching for you to come and save me
But instead I sabotage.
Digging my own grave.
Hiding my emotions in dirt and camouflage.
I know better.
You know better.
We know better.
But it's whatever.
Gotta be the bigger person.
Being the smaller person feels better.
It's safer.
My feet are closer to the ground when I f
                                           a
                                            l
                                              l.

Then I don't have to show how I feel
When you don't call.
I don't gotta say I miss you
Or that I'm sorry anymore.
When I could say I hate you,
I fell for a whore.
I know I'm lying.
You know I'm lying.
You started the lying.
Why are we still lying?
Tears are the blood stains
When the heart is dying.
I s p a c e out
While looking out towards the window
Thinking about you.

But you'll never know…

DIARY ENTRY NUMBER 1 #45

These are the diary entries of the broken hearted.
I just have to say, I don't know where it all started.
Maybe it's the broken condom wrappers
Under the kitchen counter.
Maybe it was the Victoria's Secret bags
That wasn't ours.
I honestly don't know.
I count the days, minutes and hours.
All I can say is I'm sorry.
We both know that sometimes words don't really matter.
You told me to show you more.
I just let the dream shatter.
I treated you like you weren't who you were;
My heart.
I let my heart turn black and my love walk away,
Just to watch everything fall apart.

DIARY ENTRY NUMBER 2 #46

The immature life decisions
Of an immature 20 something.
Only one real life goal;
Never to be caught bluffing.
He knows obvious things,
Like girls come about a dime a dozen,
And will enter your life like buses-
Miss one and the next one coming.
Sadly, immature 20 somethings can't gain wisdom
Until after the fall.
It was when I treated my ex fiancé like just another woman
That I lost it all...
But gained wisdom.
You can't treat the one
Like just another one.
I'm hoping and praying you ain't the one.
I'll probably never find another one-
Like you.
A wise man knows that the phrase, *"I'm sorry!"*
Doesn't even matter with me and you.
That's like trying to repair a broken home
With glue.

OLD VOICEMAILS #47

I just downed a couple of shots of Bacardi.
Damn I really miss the feel of your body...
Love watching it sway.
I still think about you on my day to day.
Baby girl, you was always bad enough to steal me from my past ways
But in the past is where your spirit stays.
Where my mindset decays
And temptation plays.
I wanna be different from our time alone.
Honestly I just have a hard time being alone.
I really do wanna be more faithful and
Stop letting my manhood roam.
I need a place where my head can rest.
I need a girl who is obviously better than the rest.
We both know relationships are hardest when we're honest.
Lies are easier to digest.
The lies we tell can preserve happiness if you let it,
But self destruct relationships in a matter of seconds if you forget it.
Your skin taste like strawberries cuz of your lotion... I didn't forget it.
Our relationship was just a lot of work... *I wish you didn't quit it.*
At night I relive it.
Now my dreams I envy.
When it was just you and me,
Was there any love... and I do mean any?
I stress about it plenty.
Regrets are embedded within my past ways.
Along with the fear of being alone and seeing it drag me away
Like the seaweed on the beach engulfed inside the crashing waves.
I can still see you walking away.
I whispered for you to stay.
You didn't hear me so you just left like the day.
Still can't handle being alone.
I always felt alone.
I'll chase anything like it's my last breathe... just to not feel alone.
...Damn I need more liquor.

60

FALSE FANTASIES TILL WE WAKE UP #48

Listening to phrases that drake wrote.
If you wait too long the good ones do go.
We should have been married ages ago.

We played house in Atlanta where the trees grow,
And the peaches are,
And everybody smiles to say hello no matter who you are.

We even smiled to our own faces like we know who we are...
But never truly did.

Thoughts changed.
People changed.
Feelings remain the same.

Wish our problems were plain
Like you snore too much
And I lift the toilet seat up.

It's deeper than that.
Feels like we broke our pact.

Never deleted the date in my phone.
Stuck wondering where everything went wrong.

Sometimes I wish you left me alone.
Sometimes I wanna go home
But home is where the heart is.

Now we are dearly departed.
I was left homeless while wondering where your heart is.

I feel like I loved you more than you loved me.
I feel like I need you more than you need me.
I feel like you fed and ate from my energy.

At times you inspired me.
At the end of the day we picked up the pieces;
The war is over, wave the white flag and let's make our peaces.

You go left, I go right and we travel wherever fate leads us.
Let us pray that the clicking clock never defeats us.

Old pictures making it look like we should get married
But I'm afraid of commitment, rings are too scary.

Old text messages saying I can't wait till we're married
But now I got new distractions that I think about barely.

MY PRIVATE PITY PARTY #49

Love is my religion
Even though I'm sinnin'.

Roaches burn through my floor
When I over think decisions.

Old ashtrays,
Only filled with memories,

So Imma try and forget every single thing
That made you leave.

I'm smoking weed
That would garner noise complaints.

Alcohol and conflict
Caused them 20 cups in my kitchen sink.

I smoke to ease the pain
But you leaving was the only thing that changed.

Feelings edged in stone

So they still remain the same.

Alcohol's my make up
To conceal the pain.

Eventual mistakes
That feel like innovations.

Sleeping with these new girls
With you as motivation.

I was the type
To fall for temptations.

So I'll invite them new girls to my private pity party
To forget all about you.

Till the high wears off
And I wake up with thoughts about you.

Pills placed on my tongue.
Smoke within my lungs.

Running from forgotten love
Till I become undone.

RUNNING FROM YOU #50

I bit the apple.
Fell to my knees.
I didn't wanna hear no broken promises
Or empty words like "please."

I needed something to help me cope
On my own.
Think I used up every drug
People use so they don't feel alone.

All the women I used up
Just so I didn't feel alone-
But I am alone
Inside of my own home.

I left when you left
Like that's something to condone.
I don't think I've even learned a single lesson.
It's depressing.

Popped too many pills
To keep from stressing.
I'm faded.
I feel me fading.

There was a life that we were making.
Now look at what I have created.
So many things I've used
To keep me sedated.

I can see me,
Dying.

ANGELA MY ANGEL #51

Angela my angel
You didn't deserve that.
I don't deserve to be loved
... I already knew that.
Lost in a mental state
Where nightmares appear in the light.
Drifting so far away
That wrong can only be seen as right.

Angela My Angel
You didn't deserve that.
You bought the dream
... Just so I could sell you a lie right back.
I just wanted to protect me
Sadly, I ended up hurting you.
Purely because of my past
And a clouded point of view.

Angela my angel
You didn't deserve that.
You wanted to be loved
... I just gave you a heart attack.
I made you my pit stop
Towards the heart break hotel.
I told you, "You were where I wanted to be."
The difference between my truths and lies are getting hard to tell.

Angela my angel
You didn't deserve that.
You just wanted all the love letters
... My heart couldn't write back.
That wasn't cool.
You didn't deserve me turning you jaded.
Turned into another lost girl
Only out there for revenge while getting faded,
But Angela, you know, you didn't deserve that.

Angela my beautiful angel
You didn't deserve that.
All you did was love me
... I didn't love you back.
Probably doesn't matter
But I really thought I did.
I just used you up like a drug
Because of the one I'm trying to forget.
But Angela, you know, you didn't deserve that.

TO STILL BE IN LOVE #52

I just wanna do wrong
But make it feel right.
What's done in the dark
Comes with an eventual spotlight.

Its getter harder and harder
Just to go out at night.
Cuz your paparazzi ass friends
Wanna tell you bout mine.

Almost like you was mine but you really ain't.
You always wanna go around in public
Acting like you a saint.
Bitch you cheated too!

Sorry if I come off a bit rude.
But you the one that made it this way
So you're not the one I'm forced to report to.
Freedom should feel better
Than it does.

Maybe it feels that way
Because I never really was.
A slave to how my heart feels
After being crumbled up.
It really makes you feel like shit
To still be in love.

OUT OF MY MIND #53

I saw the writings on the wall,
Baggage on the shelf.
I rather be right here screaming and arguing with you
Than be with someone else.
I think I heard that in a Kanye song.
Now I hear the sentiment echo in the hallways when I'm by myself.
You never acknowledge that it's coming,
But you always know when it's felt.
I rather self destruct with you
Than be with someone else.

THE DRIVEBY #54

I drive by your house sometimes.

Ok, I'm lying.

It's on my way to school so I see it all the time.
I stare it down from the corner of my eyes.
I have it perfected to the point where I'll never
Crash but I may cross the lines
On the pavement.

You're too far away to hear my statements
But I felt yours.

Those last sentiments before we became just a blur
Upon the timeline of the universe.
We need to converse, but we don't.
We could have done better, but we won't.

I replay our arguments a hundred times just to realize we don't know what we want.
We just knew that heartbreak can haunt.
So we just constantly lied to each other like when
I said I was ok and you did too.
Regardless, those memories are stuck to haunt our rearview.

Mental breakdowns
Live within the devil's playground
Where my feelings pound the pavements of my mental cavities.
We had a fuck it mentality.

That's destructive still.
I don't wanna poison my eyes by looking at that house but I
Probably will.

MY ROOM #55

Roaches move through my room.
Weed has me stuck in my room.
Hennessy bottles decorate my room.

You are not in my room.
I miss having you in my room.

You used to bring me drugs to my room.
You were the strongest drug in any room.
Your naked body invades the connection I have to my room.

I can't live here anymore in this room.
I see the stains through the carpet of this room.

Drug residue paints over the broken promises in my room.
Broken bottles with empty spirits are starting to fill up my room.
My broken spirit still belongs to you and this room.

Too many thoughts of you are trapped within this room.
It feels like if I ran away I would still be trapped inside this room.

FACELESS TATTOOED TEARS #56

Tired of these
Tattooed tears.

They only showed up
Cuz you're not here.

Pain grows stronger over time.
We don't even act like peers.
Just lost souls
Going in different, haphazard directions.

Looking at me
Like it wasn't my bed you slept in,
How dare you!
Lost in thought, lost in space, just lost,

On my way to Planet Lost.
Waiting for the set time for lift off.

Earth has nothing else for me
And reality is flawed.

Because my former best friend
Won't even answer the phone when I call.

Who am I kidding,
I won't even dial the number to call.

Just random, faceless numbers
Saved in my phone now.

Tattooed tears
Means it's harder to smile now.
A relationship has died

Creating two strangers.
Two souls, once connected, were destroyed
And now the world can't get much stranger.

YOU'RE HERE WHEN YOU'RE GONE #57

I can feel you fading away,
Like the incense that invaded this room.
I wanna say it feels safe to say you're gone,
But I can still see you so it's never safe to assume.
I can still see the way you strut around the house,
When you bought new shorts for the summer.
I can even hear the cute way you snored,
Deep within your slumber.
I would never wake you.
In the winter time we shined,
I could still feel your breathe in that log cabin.
When you said you were mine.
But now,
I slowly feel you fading for your exit.
But I still feel your presence around me.
Ain't that some shit.
My heart, soul and conscience
Are having a conference and I can hear the chatter.
I'm still in love.
Not that it matters.
I'll probably get over it...

GENERATION GAP #58

The kids born in the 80s and 90s
Don't believe in religion or politics
Because of what happened to the kids
Born in the 60s and 70s.

Millennials won't get married
Cuz their parents never were.
They just get into situationships, hoping not to get played,
Because that's all that their parents ever did.

Some of the babies born in the 20s, 30s, 40s and 50s
Were born just to die.
Born into lynchings, murders, drugs and wars.

And some of the kids born in the 70s, 80s, 90s and 2000s
Are still being born just to die.

Born into police lynchings, murders, drugs, wars and dirty politics.

9 DEAD INSIDE THE CHURCH WALLS #59

My Heart is broken.
My Heart is weary.
My Heart is tired.
My Heart is hurting.

My Heart is screaming out loud
To the clouds
Right now.

Were we forsaken?
Are we forsaken?
Has God left us in the dark?

Or lost somewhere with weapons that are sharp
To bleed the tales of our aching hearts?
Is prayer working? I am not for certain.
9 left dead on the church floor while talking to God
While an evil spirit prayed with them for an hour before the barrage

Of bullets pierced the skin of the Lord's followers.
Beautiful souls whose bodies are now being prepared for their
Mournful flowers.
Prayer should redeem and replenish

But the devil struck before prayer was finished.
Hate shot through my soul so fierce it was draining,
So fierce that only sorrow was remaining.
I've never felt so lost in this ugly world.
Alone and bare in this God forsaken world.

My Heart is broken.
My Heart is weary.
My Heart is tired.
My Heart is hurting.
My heart is screaming out loud.
9 dead inside the church walls, gunned down.

THEY TOOK MY COUSIN FROM ME #60

They took my cousin from me.
They drove up, busted shots, and sped off.

He wasn't even the right target.
He was just there, bullets hit his skin, and he fell...
He turned from a soul into a corpse in a matter of seconds.
He was breathing, then got cold,

And it all stopped...

My whole family is still in shock.
News spread, they heard, and tears fell.
You took my cousin from me.
They drove off, police didn't come, they won't even solve it.

THEY GOT AWAY WITH SOME
WRETCHED, DEMONIC SHIT...

His daddy wants em,
In cold blood, on cold concrete, feeling cold.
We want our family member
Talking, laughing and breathing.

But he never will again...
Cuz they took my cousin from me.

DOES IT MAKE A SOUND? #61

If a black child dies in the woods
Does it make a sound?
What about on concrete.
No questions asked when the police meet...

Just rounds.

It's bullets first
Because they need protection too.
But one more question,
Who protects us from you?

We'll be an endangered species soon.
Life's a gun-range and we're target practice.
More killers and villains these days
Wearing badges.

It's crazy sometimes.
"Will I be next?"
I ask myself sometimes,
"Do I need a white mask or a bulletproof vest?"

Can't wear hoodies when it's cold
Or even use our pockets.
Death around the corner
Whenever they stop us.

They're not all bad.
That's what makes it worst.
I'm not willing to find out who's who
Just to ride off in a hearse.

It's their universe,
Don't it feel like that sometimes?
A lot of us are packed in jails
But who pays for their crimes...?

ASPHALT GRAVEYARDS #62

I am the endangered species whose soul plagues the earth.
I am the creature crawling on his knees trying to make it all work.

My eyes have seen everything that was delivered through a filter.
My body felt everything with malice as delivered.

They left me on the ground and told no one to go near me on this concrete.
I heard my momma scream out for me as if I heard it through a pair of Dre Beats.

Tears and blood left my shirt soaking
With bullet holes that kept the pain wide open.

Am I my brother's keeper?
Or Am I my brother's deceiver?

No I am just a product of a dying environment.
A creature that they are killing and keeping it quiet-

Until we riot.

Then they shame the victims who aren't killing
And mixed them in with the victims who are.

Black on black crimes are permanent scars
Used as a reason to wipe out an entire race that they wanted gone anyways.

Beaten pit bulls that are being cattle prodded in their cage
To fight while their city is being set ablaze,

Like *Gone with the Wind*, the city is burning down and they're blaming you.
The initial victim that was killed in the middle of the street running to get home to

A mother that always said, "Running the streets will haunt you."
Black kids are killing other black kids, this is true.

But it shouldn't be a crime to just be running,
especially just to get home.

It damn sure shouldn't equal a couple of bullets
to his back and dome.

So don't blame me while my city is burning
and destroy my character for the trial.

I was never a perfect human being but I am still my momma's child.
I deserved to come home that night instead of lying on the street.

Bullets pierced my temple and terminated my ability to breathe.
Now my name becomes one with the other names used for protest.

These asphalt graveyards are hard for the city to digest.
In a constant state of fear as we ask, *"Will I be next?"*

THE HOPELESS DREAMER #63

I wish love reigned all
    But hatred lives inside us
        And inspires law.

AMERICA THE BEAUTIFUL #64

America the beautiful,
Home of the brave.
Built off the backs of tortured
And dead slaves.
Built off the backs of ostracized immigrants
With dismal pay.
Built from ambitious regimes
That took everything they decided was theirs to take.

DNA PSYCHE #65

I am African by history not by culture,
The record was never chosen.
I am American by culture not by history,
I was stolen.

"Every man was created equally."

They wrote while house slaves were in the room.
But if Africans weren't people due to their skin
Then there's no paradox to assume.
These African Americans aren't citizens, nor people.

Can't you tell from the innocent convictions in the court room?
Or two years for murder.
Couple months for good behavior.
Good cops defending bad cops,
That's loyalist,
Extremist behavior.

If they are not all bad,

Then why are there dead bodies in broad daylight
And blood on the leaves.
Remember the initiative,
Once freed, they wanted us to leave.

Like the red man and brown man
I feel the evil, we've seen the greed.
Institutional racism.
Mental Slavery.
400 plus years on the noose.

We
Still
Can't
Breathe.

You can't replace all those buildings.
Lit trashcans on fire to throw at cars.
But you can replace
Trayvon, Michael, Walter, Tamir, Sandra, Alton, Philando, ...

But we still feel their scars!

"BLACK PARANOIA" #66

Black kids walking down the street
Is it subliminal?
I mean they did say that
Trayvon was a criminal.

Terror in the way they walk the streets
These days.
Evil in their appearance
When they want to catch a bus or a train.

But good job now the cops are surrounding them.
They're stuck.
Whoops, the gun slips,
Is it good or bad luck?

But hey, they were probably high anyways.
Lost in the clouds.
Bullets piercing their skin.
Now they're stuck in the clouds.

Filled with bad intentions
Man they won't even smile.
Anytime they riot
Proves they're violent and wild.

Fitting the description
Skinny, fat, short, large
Or Black...
Is that why the police stopped all them cars?

Short hair, long hair, black hair, blonde hair
If the description is wide, it makes the criminal less rare.
Staring at the barrel of the gun is American
But it ain't fair.

Police shout, "Freeze!"
Now the suspect's on their knees.

"You wanna know what happened haa,
Silly nigger please.

Shut up, sit down, and pass them IDs.
Your backpacks too, better pray we don't find nothing in these."
Snapbacks, jays, and tanks
Do they fit the description?

Another nigger dead but nothing was found missing.
"Black Paranoia."

THE LOST SONNET WRITTEN ON BLACK PAPER #67

Violence hits the city swift.
I just watched my little cousin planted in a grave.
The black plight is written like the black myth,
Nobody will here you scream anyways.
Little black bodies lay still with red stains on the ground.
Little black bodies swing in the wind.
This is a Christian country and I can see it all around.
Violence plagues the country so we are living in sin.
They are telling us to get over it nigger
Or that it's our fault.
But I don't care who pulls the trigger
I can't lock this pain in a vault.
My people living like refugees.
Patiently waiting for somebody to bury me.

DEAR MR. ORANGE #68

I shouldn't have to explain to you
Why my life matters.
Neither should you feel offended
That it does.
I'm not out to get you
I'm just here to defend me.
I do get jealous of your oxygen
When I'm the one that can't breathe.
We are the lonely step child
That America forgot to feed.
But I don't hate you
I just ask for the same back.
I just wanna feel like a citizen
In the place I was born in.
The place my grandfather went to war for,
Until he came home to the people he fought for
And was considered just a nigger...
Feels so long ago
Yet some sentiments remain the same.
I shouldn't live where I live
And still feel afraid.
People have their front doors unlocked around here,
Yet I leave the house in fear.
If I make the wrong false step
Then my momma will be in tears.
My name will just be a hashtag
And my flaws will be news worthy
Like I am not a human being who deserves justice!
So yes my life matters
Even if that makes you feel uncomfortable.
I'm uncomfortable every day
But I know you weren't wondering.

LIVES MATTER #69

All lives matter...
Just stop letting the killers go that kill the black ones.
Yes, paid vacations count too.
Through the police was the first time I've seen a gun.
I was completely innocent,
Still, I felt scared.

All lives matter
But I still think they don't care.
I didn't die
But that shouldn't be a surprise.
Red and blue cop lights
Shouldn't signal my demise.

Sirens, yelling and gun shots
Shouldn't be the last sounds I hear.
Feels like they're trying to meet a quota
With the death rate this year.
Feels like I'm losing all my peers
And strangers that look just like me.
Walk, talk, act and dress
Just like me.

I follow the law
More than likely.
Walk closer to the ground
So I don't feel threatening or mighty.
My skin tone is fierce.
Some would consider scary.

All lives matter
So inform the judge, police and citizens too.
I don't wanna be murdered with the narrative of suicide
Being delivered to the public and delivered to you.
Trying to block out the dark times
And yes I've had a few.

But nothing's worse than seeing a young black kid dead
By anyone's hands and my momma telling me, "That ain't news."
I wanna trust the law but there are just too many bad reviews.

Sadly,
I'm not the only one that shares this point of view.
And trust me America,
We also wish it wasn't true.
But you can't turn a blind eye
When it's happening to you.

WHAT YOU CRYING FOR? #70

Fox and CNN asked me why I'm sad
When someone that looks like me dies...
I guess humanity is a foreign idea to the news contributors.
Well I'm sad because it is no mere human beings
Job to decide if I'm still alive.
But in this current climate,
I constantly doubt if I will survive.
We are being hunted for sport
By black cops and white cops,
Red ops and blue ops,
The killing may never stop.
Been like this since the dawn of time,
We've just been the targets for a couple of centuries now.
I think I may have cried out all my tears
Seeing my brothers and sisters silenced and gunned down.
Damn near lost the strength in my voice seeing killers
Being acquitted with the ignored evidence in their trials.
It's completely legal to kill my people.
Ain't no cracks in the system!
We always knew it was legal....
The news wants a bird's eye view to our mindsets
While taking away our humanity.
Saw and ignored our pain
And deemed it insanity.
Rioting is the screams of unheard people
And over the centuries we've been left voiceless.
Too many bodies left on those concrete graveyards,
Lifeless.
We kill ourselves everyday
While police are killing us everyday.
Some get in trouble and receive paid vacations
While colored boys are committing the same exact crimes and are locked away.
Constant reminders of how long ago it was
Since America owned slaves
Just to mask the presence
Of slavery in the present day.

WHY GOD ? #71

Why you letting them kill us God?
Black people love you.
Only pictures of Martin and Obama
Placed next to you.

Our parents raised us on you
Since we were in preschool.
Our parents said, "If we followed you
The devil will never win the war."

All these deaths in the news lately
Are leaving battle scars.
Little dead babies everywhere,
Dads and moms left in the street,

Teenagers
Put to sleep.
Bullets pierce the skin.
They treat us like a piece of meat.

A statistic,
A number,
One false step
Towards eternal slumber.

My mama said for you,
"There is no such thing as a tall order."
Sadly, it seems like the devil has to be in the lead
And it's like the 4th quarter.

Please let us quit dying for nothing.
They shoot us if we stay
Or start running.
This goes for cops

And our own kind as well.
We follow your guidance

To avoid hell,
The crazy thing is we living in it.

Just one false step away from "hanging myself in a jail cell."
Or getting shot in a church
Where you reside.
I thought that it would be here

Where I could hide.
Not even safe in my own community
I prayed you would stop it and life could be just.
I wished, hoped, and prayed

You could just come and save us.

SIMILARITIES #72

They killing us.
We killing us.
They hurting us.
We hurting us.
They gave us drugs.
We serve em up.
Things are not just.
Morally corrupt.
We scream for change.
We do not change.
We scream in pain.
They watch us the same.
They riot...
The news is silent.
We riot...
They can't stay quiet.
They are scared.
We are scared.
These days are rough.
When will enough...
Be enough!

I SAW THEM TAKE IT FROM ME #73

They took my brother from me.
They took my cousin from me.
They destroyed everything that I believed.
Then later on I received
A narrative they would force feed

To the urban communities.
They took my sister from me.
Because of you, I have no auntie.
Brainwashed, annihilated, rebuilt and deceived.
Lost in the world with no self worth or humanity.

I'm brash to force my place in the universe, you see.
But before there was a place for you, there was a place for me.
Took away my glasses, so I couldn't see.
Took away our sight and memory
So we wouldn't believe.

They took my father from me...
They took my mother from me...
Threw my father in jail for centuries.
Then gave my mother drugs because there were brain cells to deplete.
They took my loved ones from me.

Dead and gone are all my homies.
And now you sit here and ask me why I'm angry?
You sit here and tell me I have no right to be angry.
You told us to shuck and jive and there will be a place for thee.
We sit in this cage hoping to be set free.

Today, right now, we will be free.
And nobody's help will we need.
I'll stand up and shout, "Follow me!"
Because I wanna be free...
Before the sniper's bullets come down

And they take my life from me.

POISONOUS #74

Can't use my piece without the fingers I use to represent peace.
There's a war outside in these streets
That could rival the one in the Middle East.

Yet the ones that are giving out money for them to regroup and recoup
Are lacking the funds for our neighborhoods like they lacking funds for the troops.

What is this hell that we living in that we comfortably call the truth?
Cops out here needing bullet proofs

Cuz they are still killing our loved ones and hiding, if not
Disregarding, the proof. Hold up though, a black man killed
My uncle as he laid there slain.

He was no angel, he had drugs to slang.
Always said he had two bullets dedicated to the revival gang.

Young niggas that feel defined by the colors they bang.
But no matter how we die, it's still all the same though.

Justice is not black and white but was promised to us though.
Yes the American Dream lied and only gave it to those that they deemed worthy.

Lady Justice's eyes seem blurry. So you saying I can only get
Justice if the killer looks like me?

Without a badge, then maybe they can hear our screams.
That badge, that gun, makes it so they can't hear our pleads.
Justice or else... please.
Justice was never ours since they sewn in them stars.

We needed or else a long time ago before the black race is just a
Mirage. A figment of the history book's imagination
To redefine who we are.

POISONED MINDS OF THE CONCRETE JUNGLE #75

I don't wanna live like this.
Where I know there's enemies on the other side.
I wanna kill them
Because they're from the other side.
They have loaded guns
To make sure that I stop breathing.
Parents outside-
They're still preaching.
Always talking about,
"We can stop the violence!"
No we can't,
Peace has been silenced!
So many friends, brothers and cousins
Been taken from me!
The temperature is hot outside
And it's getting ugly!
So much money spent to fight in wars
But it's a war zone out here and we're still poor.
I don't wanna live like this.
When death is something you look towards.
Old heads telling me,
"This is a lifestyle that you can quit."
But if the enemy still wanna kill me
Then don't force feed or try to sustain me off some bullshit!
Fuck your empty solutions!
Fuck your after school special type narrative!
Ain't nobody trying to hear that
Where I live,
The gun shots and cop sirens are too loud...

I AIN'T FROM IT, I AM OF IT #76

Man I ain't with that lifestyle, that gangbang.
Still got some niggas slain.

Their daddies, uncles, cousins selling or on that crack rock,
I'm on that same block.
Windows down blasting Tupac
With my eyes out looking for dirty cops

So my life won't end today.
Looking to where the ops stay.
Niggas in my hood need a weekend get away
But all they got is some weed and an AK

If they lucky...
They just killed my nigga Lucky.
I guess his nickname didn't fit.
The killer was paid a visit.

Funeral was yesterday, I didn't go.
I hear the guns spray, late at night, outside my window.

I duck every time.
These bullets could come for you anytime.
Bullets ain't got no name.
The hood got broke and rich off cocaine.

It's a damn shame but they had to do it.
Raised off of the influence
From the older younger kids.
We examined every single thing they did.

Still wasn't my shit,
Don't mean I turned a blind eye to it.
Don't mean I didn't get Jordans from it.
Or my morals from it.

I am of it. I just don't wanna die from it.

SURVIVOR'S REMORSE #77

If you live, I die.
We are all crabs in a barrel trying to survive.
But who provided the barrel anyways?
Too late, another crab was eaten alive, slain.

IF IN POLICE CUSTODY #78

If in police custody,
No I did not commit suicide.
But if in police custody,
I am more than confident that I will surely die.
When we need you,
Where are you to be found?
Please do your job.
That doesn't mean leaving little black bodies on the ground.
We are in constant fear
Of police brutality.
To serve and protect
Seems to be a lost mentality.

TARGET PRACTICE AMERICAN #79

They killing us all man.
Black men and women.
When it's a black man,
They can just say he was large and threatening.
Usually don't have guns or drugs on us
Like it's the only thing missing.
So why not help out the cause and continue planting
The evidence so we can kill the crops.
Another release with pay, poor cops.
When it's black women, that's obvious, they wanted to die
In police custody committing suicide.
They talk too much and we don't even lie
And now you're expecting us to testify.

We told you the story.
It was sorta peaceful, not gory.
Now where's the badge and the glory
And please dead this "We just killing cuz we feel like it..." story.
They're killing us all man.
Black women and black men.
All lives matter but we barely feel human,
Don't even bring up American.
The land of the brave and free,
But the police are killing people that look just like me.

FRUSTRATED AND SCARED #80

White cops are racist.
Black cops favor self hatred.

This ain't a reality I wanna grow up nor stay in.
Grew up learning the world is a horrible place.

Then we get a little high to gain a little escape.
You get a little older screaming fuck they side till things change.

But that just leaves them madder so they kill us anyways
To receive them toilet tissue soft sentences that will let
Them out in a couple of days.

So it just sounds like we just complain
Because the cycle remains the same

With only thing changing is the face to blame.
Pain is displaced but always remains.

Feels like we were born victims,
Rewritten history with force fed futures and definitions.

THIRSTY PEOPLE'S CONVERSATIONS #81

I was from the land where the water was drying up.
And she's from the land where the water was poisonous.
We talked for hours about how the laws towards the poor were unjust.
I shared with her conspiracies about how they rounded up
And killed the homeless for a better view... MY GOD... it was blood lust.
I think we're next up.
We are hated because of our skin.
Worth more than gold is our melanin.
We have laws but no morals.
We went to war for oil
And planted an American flag right in the middle of the turmoil.
We living in crazy times.
I still remember Columbine.
Mass shootings happen every week.
This is not a war for the weak.
I've seen dead homies lying in the streets,
I heard songs about the blood on the leaves,
And read of the murderous trees.
Ghosts with ropes coming for people
That looked just like you and me.
Now that's frowned upon.
That doesn't mean you can't rewrite your wrongs
Or ignore when blatant wrongs are still being done to our young,
Our old, our mothers, our fathers, our daughters and our sons.
Shouting don't take away our guns;
I'm asking for pure water to run so we can take showers.
Poor people are being economically devoured
And chewed out. Then put right back on these desolate,
Dehydrated streets for shoot outs.
I was from the land where we prayed for floods
And she was from the land where the drinking water equaled blood.
Either way we're dying of thirst, That's what she told me.
"Baby we are people dying of thirst."
That's what she told me.

THE SUFFOCATION COMPLEX #82

Woke up scared,
Went to sleep scared.

Police raising the death rate with their quotas every year.
We yell out that we're in pain just for people to act like they can't hear.

Look at us strange and question every time they see our tears.
Killas in blue walking the streets without a care.

That's why we talk about police brutality.
That's why we raise hell in the streets, protest and have rallies.

Because they are locking black people up, **THAT'S REALITY.**

So if a black man kills me, he's going to jail.
If a cop kills me, he's getting a vacation with a check in the mail.

THE CITY IS BURNING; THE PEOPLE ARE DYING #83

I saw the whole city burn down in my sleep...
Woke up and the city was gone.

We're living in hell.
Now it smells like one.

They're killing us and don't even read us our rights-
Probably because we have none.

That's why the city is burning.
During the marching, the media and government didn't hear anyone.

Obama called us thugs
Like Fox news.

Media is reckless,
And yet we are the lawless ones with no rules?

The city is burning down
Like Scarlett's home town.

The fire represents our oppressed and frustrated voices,
I hope they feel the heat as we get loud.

But instead they disregard it,
While the media recklessly rambles.

The citizens feel like targets
While being reminded that they are one with
Every brand new example.

But the only response to every murder is that the police are doing their job.
The city is set ablaze

While people multiplied into a mob
Destroying the buildings like they were rocking the cage.

It was chaos before the riots, it just wasn't news.
The city's burning down and the people still lose.

So many staples in the community did the people lose.
Painted as savages as the world creates new rules.

I believe this is the definition...
Savages riot, lute and destroy buildings.

While the heroes...
They wear uniforms and perform the killings.

So I'm guessing you're gonna say that my numbers are askew,
So okay not all of em, but the number is too great to ignore.

They want to act like it's a race war
When its basic human rights that we ask for.

How can it be a war
When it's so one sided

And the losing side is so divided
And the people feel so defeated that it's only
In their neighborhood that they riot?

How is it that everyone is ready to chastise without any solutions?
Why is it that when we asked to not be killed, it's fought with no signs of restitution?

Told us we can't hold the police accountable because we're killing ourselves, like that's a resolution!

Innocent little kids dying every night and that's a problem!
Innocent people dying every night and that's a problem!

The people's anger is rising and that's a problem!
We have to walk the line and that's a problem!

We're forced to show the world that we are better
Than the circumstances and that's a problem!

Because they can kill us with no restrictions and that's a problem!
I feel like I could die tonight and that's a problem!

We don't feel like you hear us though and that's the problem!

So we riot and burn the city down tonight and now there's
A problem...

MASSA LOOKS SCARED #84

Massa scared of Karma.
Everything they did may come back and happen to them.
That's why they crack the whip just a tad bit harder than yesterday.
They understand the pain they give out
And don't want it to happen to them.
So what's inside the slave's mind?
Freedom!
I wanna be free so I don't have time to think about him.
But if you keep me from being free,
Then everything I've received could damn sure happen to them.
Couple centuries later and mothers are still mourning,
Yes a couple of years later and the city is still burning.

THE GOOD DIE YOUNG #85

I got dead homies.
Some didn't see 23.
Life feels shorter now.

I'VE CRIED MY LAST TEAR #86

I've cried my last tear
And dodged my last obstacle.
Next time you see me
You won't be happy.
Imma hold this trash can above my head, throw it,
And watch where my pain and frustration lands.
Imma hold this bottle of fire
And watch where my heart ache and despair lands.
Imma go inside this store
And steal every single thing I can.
It wasn't meant for me anyways, I was born at a disadvantage
From your vantage point,
So Imma level up any single damn way I can.
I've cried my last tear
And dodged my last obstacle.
Next time you see me
You won't be happy.
Tears turn to anger when left unattended in the dark.
Tears escalate into violence when observed but ignored.
And now it's all burning down...
I can sense the news is watching now.
I was a child yesterday
And now I'm a man.
I was a man yesterday
And now I'm a cannibal
Right where I stand.
Well Imma die anyways
So I truly don't give a damn.
This menacing monster won't crawl on his knees.
I rather stalk the earth, standing tall or die as a man.
I refuse to cry one single tear
As I walk through every single obstacle.
Next time you see me
I guarantee you won't be happy.

POST TRAUMATIC STRESS DISORDER #87

Way too many signs
Reading R.I.P.
Way too many shirts saying
Free the homies.
Childhood days waiting for them helicopter lights
So I could go to sleep.
The neighborhood night lights
Hovering over you and me.
Police sirens surround the city
But I don't feel safe.
Too many times cops yelling freeze,
The concrete smacks our face.
So many instant made laws
I didn't know I could break.
Or maybe they been here for years,
That's why we feel the hurt.
Too many times we ducked
And it was just fireworks.
Too many times we didn't duck
When they was firing first.
Black on black crime.
Racial on black crime.
Police on black crime.
Mentally insane on black crime.
It's getting worse every time.
Just feels like we're born to die.
Stamped and pushed out the womb
With targets on our backs.
If we don't kill ourselves
Then the system places us on train tracks.
Some knew.
Some didn't.
Some guilty.
Some acquitted.
Paranoid to leave the house
People die every summer.

Bullets raise the death rates
We're losing friends every summer.
Leaving school to go to church
For the funeral service.
Stood there and wanted to be a man
But was it really worth it?
"The one in front of the gun
Lives forever."
But once the blood spills through
Then they're gone forever.
Sometimes innocent people
Lose their lives.
Bullets ain't got no names...
They just fly.
It's not cool to say you're scared
But I'm scared.
They judge us out here.
It's a warzone out here.

THE TRANSITION #88

When you were younger,
You only cared about getting older.
Then you aged over time.
The world felt colder.

You sat in the snow
Questioning if you'll get any older
Knowing life could abruptly stop,
You still followed their rules.

You felt yourself age
When your homey got stabbed after school.
He survived.
Your childhood didn't.

Thought the law was there to help you
Then Zimmerman got acquitted.
Got stopped by the cops
Earlier before that,

Somebody strong armed a phone,
So the criminal description was everything black.
Was furious about it
But didn't wanna over react.

Then you found out the culprits was of Asian decent
And you were welcomed to the world with a smack.
Rap music used to be entertainment,
Now it's a guide and news letter.

Some things stay the same
Some things get better.
Used to sleep in chains
Now we just fear the weather.

The death rate rises every summer
And the city is getting hotter.
When we were kids,
We dreamed about being super heroes
That did good and lived forever.

Then we grew up
Into villains that are shooting and killing each other.
Used to love the city,
Now the city feeling reckless.

So I just started to put the age 25
On my check list.

WILL YOU MAKE IT HOME? #89

"Please make it home safely."
That's more than just a rap album,
It's a mantra
That's actually heard seldom.
"I mean of course I'll make it home safely…
Now let me run the streets."
"Of course I'll make it home safely…"
The going home service starts in the mourning at 8:43.
I really wish the guns were put away
But they're needed.
Unarmed folks getting gunned down everyday
And defeated.
What is decency
When I'm just trying to survive?
Why should I remember this,
You know why we get high.
Weed smoke
Makes the fall feel shorter.
We're all suffering
From that Summer Disorder.
I got one less family member,
They got one less friend,

People always die
That's a concrete trend.
Free him,
RIP them,
I wish that didn't happen to her,
Killed before they even learned to swim.
Some before they even learned to walk...
Some before they even learned to talk...
I can feel the grim reaper
And his scythe as he stalks.
I wish you would of stayed home yesterday
But you had to go hang.
I wish you didn't live by those colors
But you said you wanted to bang.
Cash rules everything around us
So you had to slang.
Now you're gone forever
Either dead or in jail.
Now your life is gone
And it feels like hell.
Wish it was all so different,
Hope it's not hard to tell.
I saw your body collapse.
When I sleep, I still hear you yell.
In the act of dying
You screamed for help.
I saw your eyes
And they screamed for help.
Your momma told us to make it home safely
And I said we would but now it's a lie.
We were supposed to make it home safely
You weren't supposed to die...

IF I GET SHOT TODAY #90

If I get shot today,
They'll say I fit the description.
If I get shot today,
They'll say I resisted.
If I get shot today,
My soul will be lifted.
If I get shot today,
No one will be convicted.
Please don't let me get shot today.
I see the police lights flicking.
I might get shot today,
He's nervous and his trigger finger itching...
BANG!
I JUST GOT SHOT TODAY.

GROW UP #91

You notice the change from being a child to an adult
When the season of summer changes its meaning.

Use to mean that schools out and there was no more to learn
Until you learn that your friend was shot and left bleeding...

He didn't make it.
Now you gotta buy a suit for the funeral service

And go to church for the first time on a Saturday.
You can feel adulthood surface as your childhood fades.

Less makes sense but more feels concrete.
The death of childhood innocence surrounds me.

Watch it
Bleed.

THE DEATH OF INNOCENCE #92

Part of me died when you died.
On your stomach, face down, you lied.
I saw the bullet wounds from a body still warm.
A coward, there was not one news outlet I informed.
They threatened my life and then my freedom.

Now I fall asleep seldom.

Was life really worth it?
For me to survive and for you to die, I didn't deserve it.
Somehow I pray the truth can surface.

KIDS THESE DAYS #93

How much do we trust the government...
Conspiracies made us believe they blew up them
Towers in September.
How much do we trust cops...
We treated the idea of Christopher Dorner as an urban vigilante.
How much do we trust doctors...
We self-medicate with our own drugs routinely.
How much do we trust their change...
If we didn't vote for Obama then we ain't voting.
The system is broken.
These kids have spoken.

CHANGE #94

You was taught hope
Like that was realistic.
They keep saying things will change
Like hate is simplistic.
Old movies talking about
Cops shooting niggas.
On the news yesterday
Was a cop shooting a nigga.
I remember the first time I learned about the world changing
Because of Dr. Martin Luther King.
Then I heard about a lynching on the news.
I couldn't bare to imagine his body swing...
Then they showed it.
Footage leaked onto the internet.
The little girls that were murdered in that Birmingham Church
Is engraved in our history so no one could ever forget.
9 shot dead recently in a South Carolina Church
Has me thinking if I will be next.
Can God even save me
When he couldn't even save us from slavery?
History repeats itself
So I still feel the effects daily.
They're still feeding us hope
Like things can change.
A black man is in his second term as president
With his citizens still viewed as animals that should be caged.
I know it has gotten better
Because there is a black man in office.
That's not an excuse to ignore
All those black bodies in coffins.
Young and old,
Feels like the same story being told
Since the history books first documented
Slaves being sold.

CONSTANTLY SCARED #95

Scared that there isn't a God
And I just waited for things to get better.

Scared that there is a God
And on Judgment Day he tells me I should have believed better.

Paranoid that I'll die before I am able to find out.
History and society dictates that people die that look like me.

From the lost ones whose names are written in blood on concrete
To ancestors who were lost at sea.

I fear for my life more
As I grow older.

What if I get caught up in the wrong colored territory
Or if I just get pulled over?

I'm scared cuz your 20s shouldn't feel like a death sentence
And some of my teenage friends didn't even get to make it over.

Hoping they're watching over me
Until it's over.

THE CYCLE CONTINUES #96

Pac is dead and Brenda's baby is all grown up
In the same damn place that made Brenda give it up,
In those dumpsters that had multiple generations messed up.
I mean this, a lot of babies been screwed up.

The value of life has been screwed up
While police roll through the neighborhood in army trucks.
Baghdad ain't got shit on us.
We living fucked up.

Ain't shit pretty and it seems like they just don't care about us.
Cube told us
In 1991 and we still lost? It's fucked up!

Baby gangsters run the city while they old heads are locked up.
Got guns in the nursery in case they wanna meet up.

We don't like them and they don't like us.
Police look exactly like the ops to us.
Police want us in cold blood just like the ops does.

We don't know where to turn, it looks just like a war zone to us.
They don't put money in us!
All they do is deliver laws that are unjust.
The second amendment never meant shit to us.

Bombs over Baghdad is cool but there were guns at
Home pointed at us.
Ashes to ashes, dust to dust
We prayed hard for a system less corrupt
Even if we knew it or not.

IT'S HOT AS HELL #97

The Cops are hot.
Gangs are hot.
Tension's hot.
The city's hot.
Peace is cold as hell.

IN MY CITY #98

People pray for my city.
They don't wanna stay in my city.
Won't even look this way towards my city.
All they wanna do is chastise my city.
Ask why gangs are destroying my city.
Police can't even contain my city.
People die EVERYDAY in my city.
Bullets fly EVERYDAY in my city.
Can't even get a job in my city.
They still ask God bout my city.
Like that's something to help my city.
They only see an abstract idea when it comes to my city.
This is real life going on in my city.
I grew up with my cousin in my city.
I had to bury him last year in my city.
Grew up with two brothers in my city.
And I'm the last one left in my city...
They only help people that don't live in my city.
Just so they can ask, "What's going on in my city?"
It's hard times in my city.
Just to live and die in my city.
Yeah I'll probably die in my city.

UGLY QUESTIONS #99

Does God notice when we die?
Dead bodies laid out on concrete.
Does God see us cry?
Defeated mothers who can barely cry out,
"That's my baby!"

RED RAIN DROPS FALL ANYWAYS
#100

Red rain drops fall through the city.
Good times are washed away.
We went from a neighborhood to a war zone,
Those dark clouds lead the way.
Leaves are soaked in the field,
Aspirations hung in the wind.
The sun ran away a long time ago,
It didn't wanna live in a city that sinned.
A city that would apologize and repent
Just to do it all over again.
Now there's just red raindrops
And pounding winds.
I think the weather is speaking to us.
I think God forgot about us.
Or he sees everything just to wonder
If we could survive in an environment unjust?
I think he knows the answer but watches us
Anyways.
He continually gave us the benefit of the doubt
Anyways.
He blessed us
Anyways.
Black folks pack up the church
Anyways.
Black churches are burnt to the ground
Anyways.
9 people were murdered inside that church
Anyways.
We still have the faith to pray
Anyways.
Red rain drops turn to violent, red waves
Anyways.

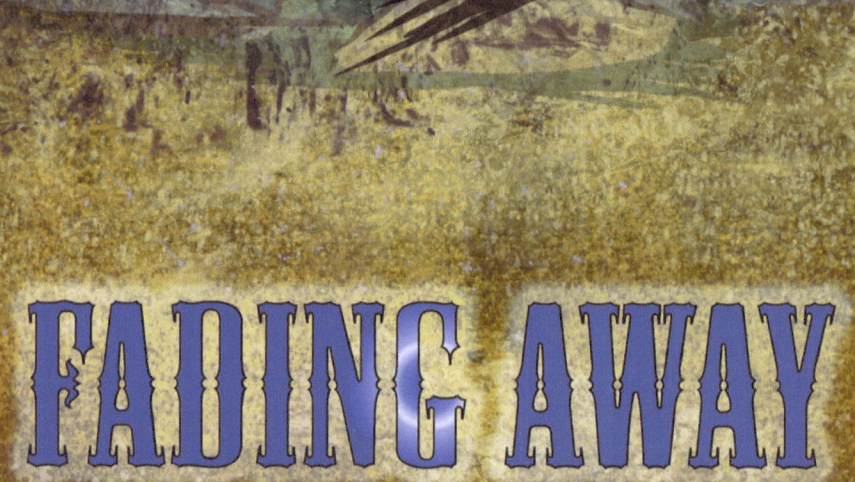

PLANET LOST #101

I feel lost in the world.
My soul drifts towards false truths.
My body is trapped in this stagnant state,
Searching for ways to be let loose.
All I want are answers
But I can barely get clues.
I look up and wonder,
Where is God in this spectrum?
I'm envious
When I hear others say they hear him.
I just feel like he's there
Like oxygen to sustain us.
But then that means he's watching us die
And letting the justice system blame us.
Especially when its law enforcement
And the jury.
All he does is watch our eyes water
When shouting out in fury.
I worry daily with clouded thoughts
When the lights are dim.
But we never blame him,
Probably not even fair to blame him.
He made us from dirt
But we devalued it and made it dirty.
People claim to be his followers
But do so with evil intent.
I know I've gleefully sinned
As a Planet Lost resident.
But I'm not the only one who lives here.
He created it for us and we made it anew.
But honestly, I still blame him
Just like I still blame you.
But don't worry too much about it
Because I still blame me too.
Planet
Lost...

FALLING SILENT TO DEAF EARS #102

This should be exciting!
I'm drinking, smoking, and writing
While my spirit is rioting.
Now there's nothing but shards of glass inside my heart.
The aftermath could tear cities apart
Like its 1992.
Nothing really changes but it feels brand new.
At least you fake it so normality can be restored.
You ignore every single thing inside you that screams for more.

INTOXICATED/HONEST THOUGHTS #103

I get high to pass the time
But don't feel bad for me.
I hope God and Karma ain't the same thing...

I know they coming for me.
I've seen everything I've ever done.
I'm still running from me.

I wonder if my fears and conscience
Are the same thing.
I see cars passing by...

Wondering if I should jump in front.
I lay and stare up on the top of this hill
Wondering what you want.

I stand up
And live within the chaos.
When the rain is pouring, thunder bangs

And lightning shocks.
My cups are always empty.
My joints are always rolled.

"I wanna be sober,"
Is a lie I always told.
Because when I'm faded...

I disappear, then I'm gone.
Keep running
Till I escape to my zone.

One puff
And for a short while,
Problems leave me
 Alone.

GOING THROUGH THE MOTIONS NUMB #104

I get high too much.
I don't feel too often.
I run away too much,
I might only stay in my coffin.
My spirit steady losing
While my mind still races
Through the moments of yesterday
Like there's some answers I'm still chasing.

THE AFTERMATH OF THE TORNADO #105

A tornado hit my sanctuary.
I'm stuck under the rubble, will you come and save me.
I've been thinking lately,
Like what if everything that happen had to happen blatantly?
Like it's a punishment, I know I read things about God burning down cities.
Alcohol has my mind racing crazy... I'm still losing.
Burnt bible pages burn slowly like my sanity... I think I'm ruined.
I don't think I belong at home.
I hate it when my mind begins to roam.
Thoughts get darker and darker within this zone.
Drugs help me feel like I'm not alone,
Till they lose their edge...
Then I'm on the edge...
Thinking, "Will I jump?"

BURIED ALIVE IN A WORLD SO UGLY #106

Don't use your religion to bury me.
To condemn my spirit because of what you believe.
Don't use Isis's Muhammad or The KKK's Jesus to destroy me.
I constantly pray for God to save me.
Every rap song warned me about a world so ugly-
It is... probably created to destroy me.
I fiend to be free
But I still can't breathe...

LIVING INSIDE THE FIRE #107

I flicked the cigarette and watched it burn to the ground,
There was gasoline all around.
I couldn't hear sound.
I was the deaf engulfed within the depths of death that surrounds...
Me.
Chaos is a place I chose to call home but forgot to blame me
When I sat on the ashes and wondered how I got here.
I laid there but didn't shed a single tear.
My spirit was frozen destroying the ability for my body to move.

BROKEN #108

I got church in the morning.
Sin in the evening.
Drugs keep me company
When religion keeps leaving.
I want more
So I'm either stealing or receiving.
My stomach is still empty
So I just keep fiending.
Looking for everything
And finding nothing.
You're born alone to die alone
So why are you still running?

SPINNING OUT OF CONTROL #109

I'll need multiple surgeries to repair these permanent scars.
I should probably go to therapy but I'll just drink till it becomes a mirage.
But I'll wake up next to the pain in the morning,
I wake up thinking I should blast my brain in the morning.
Then it'll all stop.
Last time I was stopped by the cops,
I was ok if they were to turn me into a shirt
Or a hash tag depending on my worth.
I'm worthless in my eyes
But my momma loves me or at least she tries.
I know she does but my spirit is broken.
Too many homies left their shirts soaking,
I'll pour some liquor out,
Pop all these pills that find their way towards my mouth.
I'll be in a drug coma and won't leave this couch.
I should be on a therapist's couch trying to figure it out.
I don't want to nor need to!
I don't want to vent to a person that don't know me.
Probably seen a couple of people just like me.
Seen a couple of people die and now they self medicate more than likely.
I've seen love die and spirits fly.
I'm trapped inside a deep depression and ignore the reason why.
That's how we self medicate,
Invite the drugs and ignore the things we hate.

SELF-DESTRUCTIVE VICES #110

I need somebody to love me.
I need somebody to fuck me.
Fuck me so good that you hate me.
Love me so hard like we family.
I need it all...

Just need some comfort inside these crumbling walls.
Jericho couldn't predict my downfall.
I made sure all the variables were hidden
And now I feel me slipping.
Losing me till I devour my soul.

Losing me till the villain takes control.
Lost me when the beast became whole.
So much cocaine placed upon this girl's nostrils.
I'm hypnotized from situations that are unstable and
its taking its toll.
Dead presidents cover up the dance floor.

Still acting out from the day you called me a man whore.
Dark and light liquor, I can still feel it dancing on my tongue.
Sativa rents a home in my lungs.
No love inside our hearts,
We're just brain dead zombies that are still searching for a spark.

Different pills laid out on the kitchen counter.
They should have stayed locked up in the bathroom cabinet forever.
Zombies took a hold of a whole generation
Because of this feeling that they were desperately
waiting for with anticipation.
Found liquid courage inside of this lean.

The cough syrup was found as medical use with different means.
I needed your touch more than simple street drugs
but accepted substitutes.

I accepted those substitutes knowing damn well
They don't compare to you.
I honestly don't care because I didn't deserve you anyways.
I'm self destruction's slave,

It welcomes me home
With different drugs for loan.
After I lost you, I lost my mind
And traded it in for drugs that I thought would be sublime.

So I could
Sit inside the fire.
Pretending everything
Would be just fine...
But it won't.

I LOST YOU A LONG TIME AGO
#111

I would have rather believed you were mine.
He knew you were his.
We were supposed to have a beach house,
I was supposed to have a wife and some kids.
The angel with the kiss of death
Is sealed away with your lips.
We just slowly drifted away...
I was too busy cheating to notice the change.
We both know for a fact that I am not the victim here,
Yet I feel the fatalities all the same.
You were my air, my everything.
Now I can't even find the oxygen to maintain.

WE DON'T TALK ANYMORE #112

We don't talk anymore,
We used to laugh all the time.
Can't believe we don't talk anymore,
We used to freestyle battle and rhyme.

We don't talk anymore,
Said I love you every night.

We don't talk anymore,
It was forcefully by design.

We don't talk anymore,
I texted her to say hi.

We don't talk anymore,
So I obviously got no reply.

We don't talk anymore,
I think I'm slowly losing my mind.

Since we don't talk anymore,
I watched our relationship die.
And now,
We don't talk anymore.

CRUMBLING WALLS #113

I'm trapped against this wall as these lights dim.
I hear Chance rap, "my big homey died young just
turned older than him,"
Playing in the background of my mental demise.
Sooner or later Imma have to cut all ties
To the way things used to be.
I'm still holding on to the fact that we used to be.
I sometimes forget that my friend won't turn 23.
Like... that's something I don't even have the capacity to believe.
The feeling is crazier and crazier as we get older.
Wait, a couple of years passed and now I'm older.
We graduated in the same class.
Somehow I was able to let love die young but
still can't allow time to pass.
I got books worth of pages of plans me and
the homey made together.
If I was to be real love, I still got text messages
fom when we was together.
The homey told me you would be the death of me...
But that was at 22 and now we're 23.
An age he won't see.
I feel his pain when I sleep.
I heard his voice scream and seen his body bleed.
Feelings never really go away and I mourn badly.
Couldn't bring myself to go to the funeral but drop off a bottle of Hennessy,
at least once a week, every week.
Pretty sure the undertaker's either drinking them or tired of me
And more sure that his family knows it's me.
They know they child been an alcoholic since 15.
Besides, roses wouldn't smell as sweet.
He warned me about you but I fell deeply for you anyways.
My mom prayed for him but he won't see 25 anyways.
My life is one big statistic.
Friends that weren't allowed to grow old, relationships that lacked
trust and commitment.
Chance provides the calming sounds

While I noticed that I miss you now.
Chance provides the calming sounds
While I mourn for him now.
I don't mourn well and don't do well with commitment,
I just love hard and hold onto friendships
Till they evaporate.
We all got that final date.
Mine seems to be creeping up on me as I ponder my great escape
Before it's all too late.

WHAT I LEFT UNDER THE RUBBLE #114

Like a helpless moth
To the seductive, unyielding flame.
Attracted to what's bad for me,
Near death scenarios for the soul.
I deteriorated under the rubble
Till my spirit is nothing.
I never attempted to learn.
I ran towards the destruction anyways.
Not caring if I came back alive,
So I left myself there.
Physically I am still here
But my spirit lives under the rubble crying to deaf ears.

HEART ATTACKS ALONG THE BATTLE FIELD #115

I was trying to lead you towards a
Predestined future without my glasses,
That's the blind leading the blind.
My happiness lived in your lap,
You just stood up and left that thing behind.
I got lost along the way.
That wasn't by design
But I broke your heart anyways.
You proceeded to break mine.
I might need a piece to find salvation
Inside of this losing war.
Love was lost right there on this battlefield
But was still something we looked for.
Love doesn't even know your name...
I'm the same.
Just faceless, infatuated human beings
Who eventually gave up trying to just maintain.

BARE AND VULNERABLE #116

I loved you once
But that didn't mean shit!
And trust me when I say
It didn't mean shit.
Not on my end though
Cuz damn it I did love you.
Life seemed perfect...
Even within the chaos that surrounds you.
Even when we fought
And I was mad as hell
And every argument ended with
"Go to hell!"
I wouldn't love you less,
Girl I would love you more!
I should have shown it better but I was young.
I didn't know we were at war.
Small battles
Developed into World War 5.
But on that battlefield
I didn't want our love to die.
Fidelity should have been practiced better.
Loyalties should not have been sacrificed.
Blame shouldn't equally be divided
Between you and I.
With you, I already know
I wasn't shit!
I just thought we would have time
To figure it all out and not quit.
We gave up on this!
You gave up on me!
But I didn't give you one single reason
On why you shouldn't leave!
So you left.

THE TRUTH HURTS #117

I'm tired of fucking
Why don't we just lie down and make love?
I'm tired of arguing
Why don't we ever just make up?
Too many voices in my head
And they all come with influence.
I dreamed of a life with you
Filled with happiness and affluence
But we can't build from this relationship
That we got.
Love is never gone in an instant.
It just slowly rots
Until you both finally admit
You can't stand each other.
But we got way too deep
When we stopped using rubbers.
Don't have any kids from the confusion
Only left with mixed feelings.
Mixed drinks aren't allowed
Only hard liquor for the healing.
I wanted to be your hero
And instead I turned into a villain.
I wanted you to be my all
And I ended up with nothing.
You were my everything once a upon a time
And now we're nothing.

I DON'T WANNA BE HAPPY (TO RUN AWAY) #118

I've been on the road too long,
Running away from something I wanted to find.
If you were to ask me what happiness was today...
I would just tell you it's something I'm tryna leave behind.

I don't wanna be happy
Happiness broke my heart.

I don't wanna be happy,
I can't even find my spark.

I don't wanna be happy,
I was sublimely ignorant and now I'm painfully smart.

I don't wanna be happy
So Imma drive away in this car...

Until the gas runs out
And I leave it all there
And walk away from you
Just to show you I don't care.

Pointless...
But Imma walk away anyways.

I set the car on fire to see the flames burn bright
Just to die out anyways.

THE LIFE FORCE #119

Hope is the living life force
Of the human soul.
Once that last ounce of hope is gone
It taunts you as it prepares to go.
Have you seen a woman's eyes
When all hope has been exhausted?
She feels like she tried it all
As her body breaks down from exhaustion.
Well I have, that's the walking dead
While dying to live.
Desperation in her heart
While there's nothing left to give.
But she gives it all anyways
That's the power of hope.
Pain gathers your soul
But you smile in efforts to cope.
What happens when that smile is no more
And that frown shows up
Just a little bit more.
Devastating as the process devours
Eternal hopes that you stored away
Personally for your darkest hours.
Attacking you at your most vulnerable
As every moment feels fatal.
But hope can bring rejuvenation,
What a powerful life force.
But if all hope is destroyed
Not another step can be forced.

MY HEARTBEAT #120

Darling... you... are... Marvelous,
Miraculous, strong and stupendous.

Honestly you deserve all the beautiful adjectives in the dictionary.
No wait on the contrary-

Slang terms too, you're dope please remember this
Or excuse my irreverence.

You make mighty men lose their composure,
Whether high or sober,

While minds race so fast that they lose races.
You are our Helen of Troy as your face can launch a thousand ships.

I admire you more than you'll ever know.
Loved you from the first time you held my hands and kissed my nose.

Honestly I cry at times thinking of the day you won't be there
And at times I feel like you know that I'm scared.

So you act stronger, calmer, cooler, collected,
Tears may fall in the dark but sunshine brings brighter perspectives.

My mind still can't fathom why God placed down his brightest angel for us to enjoy.
I'm pretty sure, up there in heaven, He's feeling that void.

Maybe he just wants you back
But I'm selfish and he knows that.

I want you for at least another 40 years.
Through the joys and the tears,

Through the smiles and the fears,
You're vital to my being, every single part of me.

If life were a love song, you would be the perfect melody.
Please don't leave me...

A million tears shall fall
When I lose my heartbeat.

I CAN'T EVEN BREATHE #121

I CAN'T BREATHE!
I shout that at least 10 times a day.
I look around and see white walls
Slowly fading away
To a new color,
A beat down grey.
My throat won't allow oxygen to reach me,
I cannot stay.
I reach out for help
But nothing or nobody's there to help me.
All the air is leaving
Along with every single cell of my sanity.
My brain loses count of the days,
They all seem the same.
December in the cold air
Shouldn't feel like May.
I'm actually starting to see objects
Slowly melting away.
Everything I touch
Instantly decays.
Almost like it's my spirit,
I can see the air leaving my body.
I'm choking, I can't breathe...
I just really need help from somebody.

DIARY ENTRY NUMBER 3 #122

I can't afford no head doctor
So I lay down with women who give head
Like they deserve doctorates.
I close my eyes
And live with the evil till my spirit spills.
Who really needs solace anyways.
Just look happy and don't end it all
Because others may be sad if you wasted your life away...
And killed yourself.
But if you ever told those same people that you weren't happy
Then they would probably look at you
Confused, disgusted and strange.
No real answers are found at the bottom of a bottle
But my sanity is maintained for a couple of hours.
Sometimes that's really all you can ask for
When your mind loves to run losing races
That depletes your heart.
I wanna end it all isn't a real remark.

A DANCER'S SIMILE #123
(Plays Drake music in the background)

I feel like a strip club dancer on Christmas.
Watch as her body glistens.
Yeah she loves the money, that she'll never forget to mention.
They stare at her like an interactive art exhibit but nobody
Pays her any attention.
She drifts off and looks outside... the feeling's cold.
Tears run down her face but nobody cares to know.
Blood drops down from her runny nose.
She self medicates with everything, especially coke.
But this the time of year where cash rules everything,
You need to pay for bills and presents but can't afford everything.
Can barely even find a baby sitter so she just begs her mother
Who stares at her so cold she can feel the shivering
Breeze that matches the weather.
She dances for the devoted regulars,
Because on Christmas, the ballers can afford to do better.
Dancing to the soundtrack of false dreams
To men that have nowhere else to be...
She thinks, "Just like me."
Studied dance all her life but it was this stage she shined on
But the light dimming was her outcome.
Looking forward to the little time she's afforded
To cry in her bathroom
While her son is on a play date in the other room.
Young, but old enough to assume his mother
Playing with her nose powder.
One day the silence may get louder,
The dances she's done to provide for him may grow sourer.
She washes the stink off for hours in the shower.
She feels dirty... but only on Christmas when the fantasy crumbles.
No cocaine today to help her thoughts remain jumbled.
So she just feels the falls with no one to catch her...
No one to catch her.
All she wanted was love.
All anyone wants is love.
(Cuts off Drake song here)

BREAKING POINTS #124

I've seen Kurt in my rearview.
Bullets that were made for two.
Weed with some angel dust.
Love that was only lust.
Substances fog my vision
Or maybe I just don't pay attention.
Yes, I've been insane.
Engulfed by the words of Cobain.
Nirvana is the anthem
When happiness is up for ransom.
Can I get that back!
Thinking causes heart attacks.
I just need a plan from a friend
Before all is condemned
To the afterlife.
All I wanna do is write
This little letter for you...
Placed on my body in a clear eyed view.
Hopefully this way you don't think it was you.
It was all completely me.
Less and less time for me to breathe.
Depression grabbed me and whispered
That I wasn't in Kansas anymore.
Then yelled...
"LOVE
DON'T
LIVE
HERE
ANYMORE!"

TODAY IS THE DAY #125

I think today is the day
I'm going to die!
Laying here with these thoughts that won't stop.
I don't know why.
Pops told me a while back,
"Real men don't cry."
Doctors told me,
"I'm suffering through Manic Depression."
Pops told me,
"Who isn't... we're in a recession!"
Ignored it
For a couple years.
Swallowed up
Some real good tears.
Slowly distanced myself
From all my peers.
Dying inside
And nobody hears.
So today is the day
That I'm going to die.
I'm weak physically and emotionally
As I hear my pop's voice echoes, "Only the strong survive."

DYING #126

I live with this hurt,
My depleting spirit fades.
Beautiful hope slain...

EMPTY HOURGLASSES PT. 1 #127

I don't know if it ends.
I just search through my mind
To replay where it begins.
I can watch the sand falling
In the glass one by one.
Believing that it's stalling,
My life in the devil's hand
Because of some mistakes.
Some were planned.
The hamster is tired on its wheel.
I'm Moses talking to God
Screaming on that hill.
Maybe that right there
Should be my downfall.
Maybe then, right there,
I'd hope you would call.
I wish that you would be my lover,
My therapist.
I wish I could find happiness
Amongst your lips,
Those were all dreams.
Stupid pipe dreams.
I hear those screams
When I go to sleep.
Yet everything seems so calm,
So serene,
When I smile in your face.
What a stupid scheme.
I really thought I could handle this all on my own.
I tried to pray one last time
But nobody was home.
Sometimes I feel like
A motherless child
In the arms of my mom
Who hasn't known me in a while.
It's my fault.
I don't talk to her.

Thoughts locked away in a vault
Hoping if I talk vague enough
The conversation will halt.
Never wanted her to be a savior
Just to say I understand without breaking
In order to fix my behavior.
But this hurts me
Knowing it would hurt her.
The top in the glass is getting close to empty
By nature.
Wishing I didn't have to be strong
So I could be nurtured.
I lost myself
Thinking someone will find me.
Life has crushed my glasses
Thinking it will blind me
And it's right...
I can't see.
Brain dead.
I can't believe
All these tears
Within the deadly seas.
No treasures here.
Just flowers and mourners saying R.I.P.
It's the end for me
As I see the last bit of sand and my breathe leave.
I've been slowly dying for the past couple of years.
I'm just forcing my body to catch up
To my spirit and start reacting.

THE LITTLE LETTER #128

I hurt myself today
To see if I still feel.
I woke up purely to ask myself
If it's all still real.
It's all laid out in front of me

On the big screen movie reel.
Deep in the depths of my mind
Where everything stands still.
Silence
Alludes me.
So many thoughts
Escape me.
Through the sea of tears
Trapped in my eyes.
Though this sea evaporates,
Crystal clear behind the rusted gates.
Feeling trapped, it engulfs me,
Swallowed me whole.
First my anger,
Then my soul,
I lay it all down.
But in all honesty
I could never tell you.
I don't have the strength
To carry the ten pound boulders
And they get heavier by the day.
All we do is get older.
Lacking the courage to cry out loud,
I wish I was much bolder.
To scream out *"I'm hurt*
Please help me!"
But it stays inside for that's a dangerous taboo,
A man's pride won't let me.
I'd rather go away
In the end
Then worry you
My friend.
I hope you're not mad
When you read this letter.
I only said I was ok
Because I couldn't get it all together.
Now everything's unraveled
And gone forever.
Bye.

I SAW IT HAPPEN #129

I died in your arms.
You shook me saying, "Don't leave!"
I wish we talked more...

EMPTY HOURGLASSES PT. 2 #130

He's gone too young.
No he's not, he's just gone.
Never to be again,
Just another sad song.
But this hurts everyone else
When the hourglass is broken.
At least if empty from the other side
Then there are words to be spoken.
We had time to
But you robbed us of that.
Now you're gone, damn it you're gone...
You remind us of that
When I look at your grave,
I grieve and I sat.
On the harsh, prickly grass
Where you're supposed to be.
Right in front of me
That's where you're supposed to be!
Flowers representing
Everything you're supposed to be.
Beautiful and flourishing
Instead of 6 feet
Under.
Remember when you always talked about being basketball tall.
Now you're buried within the dirt
Representing the height requirements through your fall.
So no he's not gone to soon...
He's just... FUCKING... gone.
I wish I knew
What was really wrong.
He smiled to my face

And cried in the dark.
Now his grave lies to my face
And I live in the dark.
I cry in the day
And cry when it's dark.
There's a pain in my chest
That's rotting my heart.
I wish you were here.
I know that you're not.
I mean I really wish you were here
But now all I can see are pill bottles and rope knots.
I miss you every day, your smile I never forgot,
I never will.
I really wish you were here
But your spirit couldn't find the will.
I hate the phrase "he's gone too young,"
Like dying later would help.
I shouldn't have to bury my child
With him thinking he was left in this world all alone by himself.
I loved him so fucking much,
I don't even know if he knew that.
So Imma scream it to the heavens
And pray that he hears that.

THE BRIEF, AGELESS FLAME #131

One day you are here.
The next, you are forgotten.
Make life eternal!

SAVE ME #132

If I'm drowning
Save me.
Give me mouth to mouth resuscitation
Or deliver me in your left hand my sanity.
Bring to me hope
In your right.
Then I will pray to God
That you were right.
All my pains, may they wash away
In the sandy waters as I begin to write.
I sit still and stare at the beach
So that I may feel one with the universe.
I look towards God
In hopes that we may converse.
With conversations that last all night
If necessary.
Flip my hourglass so that I may start over,
I fiend for clarity
Within my existence.
I fiend for happiness,
I crave it,
Even if only I can witness.
I am selfish, yet loving.
Yet in the ocean of regret
I felt my wrists cuffing
Me towards the bottom
Of the ocean.
I screamed for help,
My body lacked motion.
So if I'm drowning
Please save me.
I've asked this my whole entire life
Wondering if you will save me?
Then I saw a hand reach out inside the sea
When I couldn't breathe.
So I stepped away from the bright, white light
Wondering where this hand will take me.

A FLOWER GREW HERE #133

A flower grew beautifully in a dessert plain.
It was forced to grow in a place that never rained.
Only harsh weather and chaos reigned.
The flower had no shelter but was still able to maintain.
The flower wasn't supposed to flourish but it did anyways.

BRAND NEW #134

There's an inch of light that breaks through,
That's the sun making its way to my heart.
Mentally, I am exhausted,
But my heart races for the blood and oxygen that was apart.
I initially looked for God to condemn me.
Instead I found your crying, smiling face.
I wanted it all to end
But this feels like a second chance with a brand new head space.

You
Saved
Me.

MOVING ON AND ON #135

Heroes are flawed and falling.
People every day are dying.
Fathers continually stop trying.
Water's drying up and nearly gone.
Police stay doing wrong.
And life keeps going on and on...
This world ain't stopping for you!

THE MEANING #136

The sun sets, the sun rises.
One soul is born while another soul dies.

It's the circle of life that keeps spinning.
It may seem to pause for a second but it will continue spinning.

Sadly some of us can't afford a happy ending.
Some of us are born into flawed beginnings.
Skeletons don't find their way towards the closet on their own.
Some of us aren't even allowed to pick a place we call home

Physically.

But spiritually,
You decide where you belong.

Self realizations explode once you hear that gong.

These bongs
Don't have the answers.

These blunts can't kill the cancers.
If I may be blunt, life is shorter than we can imagine.

Even if it feels drawn out like anime heroes fighting dragons.
We have to reach out and grab what we think the meaning is.

We have to find out what it means to live.
Live our truths and be specific.

Don't just wish they would go far away across the pacific,
They'll always be right here.

Don't live in this space second tier.
This is the main event.

The afterlife doesn't have promised rent.
Where you wanna go and who you wanna be

Is real and not for make believe.
Just gotta extend your reach

Before they give your memorial speech
With only pipe dreams of what it could have been.

When you die you want heads to spin.
Like do you know who this is?

This is a person with a spirit that continues to live
Instead of a mere soul that was dying to live.

REGRETS #137

Regrets are the stains
Of the soul.
Cleanse your rotting mind
Or die slow.

Regrets are not what you need
Or deserve.
Get rid of the poisonous source,
Its negative energy reserved.

Yet somehow they always find their way back.
They either hide in your heart or they hide in your mind.
The sad part is
The advanced human species can only use one at a time.

Some of us even think with our hearts
And love with our minds.
The flawed human psyche,
Imperfect by design.

All we do is live in denial
To try and maintain.
You can only kill regrets,
They cannot be tamed.

PEP TALK #138

Pride is learned within,
I love me because of me.
Love yours regardless.

I FOUND WORTH IN MY PIGMENT: HISTORY THROUGH MY EYES #139

We are Queens.
We are Kings.
We are Royalty.

Draped in gold,
Diamonds like rubies,
Cloths, silks, furs and satins.
In an era where we stood proudly
And years later why we said
I'm black with so much pride and so loudly.

We are Queens.
We are Kings.
We are Royalty.

We went on tours far and wide from this status
As millions wanted to observe this elegance that was shown.
Many watched in envy and draped in greed.
Knocked off our immense plateaus,
Hatred was forming
Deep within the darkness of the shadows.
But human beings were formed in God's image...
The first to walk this land were from Africa,
And they didn't look like the main cast of say
Out of Africa,
More like *The Color Purple*.
But let's continue in the spectrum of this color scheme with facts.
Jesus was brown,
God is black.
If we were to really dig deep
Within religious and historical facts,
The Hebrews I know are based in the Middle East
But the Romans and their artists didn't give a damn about that.
The white washing of heritage and history was complete within
The Middle Ages.
Present day and we don't know where our history's at.

The first human beings were created
With this beautiful dark complexion
And yet some religious doctrines tell you that the devil was black.
Or turned the people into a darker pigment as punishment,
A misdirection.
And how can people turn black
When we started this way?
Then nomads headed towards the Equator, Mediterranean, and Antarctica
Eventually becoming white as historians,
Scientists and archeologists say.
But Jesus was a Hebrew from the Middle East
So he had a little more pigment than that on his birthday.
Even though the Catholic Church's depictions
Were based more on the Pope's children and hearsay.
So therefore, to deny our melanin
Is to deny God!
And to deny God to his face,
The sinful disrespect that is too immense, too large.

We are Queens.
We are Kings.
We are Royalty.
We are Gods.
We are higher beings.

This fact comes with both disrespect
And envy.
But don't you dare ever disrespect me
By hating yourself.
I am you and you are me
And nobody else.
And if you're imaginary mixed,
Why do you have to say black last.
Like it's some type of defect
Or a curse that was cast.
This is a blessing
And we are beauty,
Not some cross to bear
Or some annoying duty.

Even though our history is the definition of pain and struggle,
We rejoice regardless.
Because we been through a lot
And are forced to celebrate the hardest.
But tell me why I learned about myself in the 7th grade
And it was all erased with negativity in high school.
Mother Africa and its people were the victims
Every time I read about someone not named Martin in high school.
Our history was erased and rewritten so we seem like the losers.
But the continent of Africa fed and replenished
Both the rapist and consumers.
Who took what's ours
And made anew?
Stomped on our concrete rose
But it still grew!
Called us terms
We did not deserve
And once we reclaimed them
Still want to try and cry foul, some nerve!

We are Queens.
We are Kings.
We are Royalty.
We are Gods.
We are higher beings.

By the way, Nigga is a word that derives from the term Negus.
Ethiopian for king.
And yet nigger was redefined to mean Black Death and ignorant
And other things obscene.
Steady changing our words, terms and history,
But what does that mean?
Ignorant because it is ignorant to even think
Someone with this pigment could be a king.
And black death because if in power,
They would retaliate for everything.
So don't let anyone that's not family say this word
Trying to come for your neck.
Unless they bow down on both knees first,
We are people to respect!

For I've been a nigga all my life,
Once ashamed, then accepting, and now proud.
How dare you define my history for me
And tell me when to shout.
I am a Negus.
A king created in God's image.

Don't you dare try and devalue me.
Priceless is my pigment!

SO PAINFUL, SO BEAUTIFUL #140

It's so painful but so beautiful
To be black.
So much history, pride
And heartache attached.
Some of us got relatives right now
That ain't here cuz they're black.
Every action in the spotlight
Means you got your whole race on your back.
That means from the politicians
To the unqualified street reporter interviews.
"First off, shout out to so and so and here's what happened was..."
Are things we wish you wouldn't do.
We wish it wasn't on TV
But they show it anyway.
Got em both,
Good and hard days.
Obama as president
Meant oppression was over.
But then it was reborn
As soon as a cop pulls you over.
Even neighborhood watchers with connections
Think they have the right for our blood.
We built this land and many others,
History gets murky and lost in the mud.
People see what they wanna be from home
To distant lands.
Got white jazz players

And rappers from Japan.
Our influences widens-
Does nothing but expand.
There's influence in the melanin
That I see on the back of my hand.
A culture that last longer
Than any trend.
We are the trends.
Whether they admit it or not
They take our beauty
But denounce it like it ain't hot.
Take it for themselves,
They have our styles
Mounted on the shelves.
We cry out...
We cry out that's re-appropriation.
Former slaves
Boxed in mentalities and motivations.
They destroyed us and beat us down,
Denied us reparations.
We are the most known
And most targeted.
Hate our people
But revere our artists.
It's so hard to be black
In the world not just America.
Some of us hate ourselves
And praise white America.
Some of us hate ourselves
And see no value in the next man.
This is the deconstruction of a race
Without any traces of a formula or laid out plans
But it was plotted...
It's just an instant made formula now.
I rather stay black
And be proud.
I may be mad
But I'll never hate my sister's child.
Rather just say
I love you out loud.

Seems like...
We're always on trial.
It's soul devouring.
Always trying to go the extra mile
To prove something,
We are exceptional
And yet we don't even acknowledge it.
We are beautiful
And we don't even accept it.
Hair like wool,
Skin like bronze to dark marble.
It's rare to look like this...
Because they are killing people that look like this...
Because the first people that were born looked like this...
Even before organized religion could exist.
We are from the motherland,
The birth place.
We were given strength
And power within us in this space.
They killing us off
And we're still here.
They wanted our history
And we're still here.
It's so hard to be black
And we're still here.
It's so beautiful to be black.
Step back in awe and you would shed a tear.
It hurts but its magnificent
To be black.
We rejoice
While others ignore facts.

I HOPE THIS SHIT OFFENDS YOU: THE REAL NIGGA MANIFESTO
#141

"All my life I had to fight nigga!"
"Every nigga is a star."
The first phrase
Combines *The Color Purple* and Kendrick Lamar.

The second phrase,
From the 70s on a shirt bold and large.
There is triumph
In these scars.

Nigga, we just wanna be free
Within these bars
Nigga.
Just know I mean it if I tell you,

"You my nigga!"

Not trying to say I own you,
But just saying I got you in my heart my nigga.
Honesty hour,
I feel more like a nigga than I do American.

Fuck 4th of July fireworks,
I just want a blunt, Kool-Aid and some fried chicken.
Even deeper than that
I just want a clearer vision.

Just be honest with me
So I know my position.
Don't tell me you love me
Then kick me in the groin.

Then eat me alive
Like you're eating steak sirloin.
Don't insult my intelligence

By saying that we all free.
That we all get justice
When we all bleed.
Will you call me a thug?
Will you stand up for me?

Are you mad that I took away
One of your weapons formed against me?
Or are you mad
Purely off of oppression and history?

It's offensive because we are loved
And we are hated.
Young lives
Get debated.

"Why should we care,
Niggas kill themselves."
So who cares if a cop kills one?
Let him walk away clean with his badge on the shelf.

Where are their marches
When the bullets come from themselves."
So really,
Who cares who pulls the trigga?

When Mike Brown and Trayvon Martin were murdered,
On the stand stood their killas
With innocent verdicts.
They basically made it a legal precedent to kill niggas.

All my life I had to fight
Nigga!
But my blackness will be center stage in your face
Nigga!

Your children and their children will be so engulfed
Nigga!
That they will start referring to themselves
As niggas!

Every nigga is a star,
I mean everyone.
Dress, talk, and act like one
I mean everyone.

We are pop culture.
But our population is only like 11 percent.
They talked about us taking over in *The Birth of a Nation*

Tracking down the madness and descent.
They would have gotten rid of us.
Put it in bills and laws
The government would deem just.

Even Honest Abe, JFK
And Smooth Talking Bill didn't fuck with us.
New phrase from Vince Staples,
"I'm just a nigga

Till I fill my pockets
Then I'm Mr. Nigga."
We had to buy our freedom
And they could still capture us and put us back.

So we take flicks of this elegance
And flash.
We reclaimed them chains with silver and gold.
Now take that!

We are defined
By racks.
We are defined
By packs.

We are defined
By stature.
Trying to make enough money
To avoid the rapture.

Wanna get paid
But in the end,
We all some slaves.
Ain't that some shit.

Trying to buy our way
To relevance.
Citizenship within this decadence.
Enough money in the right hands

Makes you white.
That's written all in The Constitution
And the Bill of Rights.
In fine print.

They can knock you down no matter who you are.
Can't hide nothing like the windows with the tint.
Imma say it one more time,
Let it sink in.

Watching the news, laws and court hearings...
I feel more like a nigga than an American.
So Imma stand up
And yell fuck it then.

I could have been the one living forever
Or the one pulling the trigga.
But instead I sit back and plot
On how Imma be that nigga, nigga.

Hold on, wait.
"Don't just call me a nigga
Unless
You call me my Negus,

Imma king."
Isaiah Rashad said that and I heard it and felt free.
Expressing the energy I needed to let freedom ring.

I'M BLACK #142

I'm black
And I'm proud.
I'm black
And I'm scared.
I'm black
And I feel like less.
I'm black
And I see more.
I'm black
And I'm targeted.
I'm black
And I'm dying.
I'm black
And my life flashes before me.
I'm black
And they expect something.
I'm black
And they're terrified.
I'm black
And my skin matters.
I'm black
And I need love.
I'm black
And I receive hate.
I'm black
With no sense of history.
But I'm black
And my history is amazing.
I'm black
And they see worthlessness.
I'm black
And I know what my worth is.
So I'm black
And I'm scared.
But I'm black
And I'm proud!

HATE #143

I don't hate you.
Hate is the action that has massacred generations.
Hate is the action
That left my ancestors on plantations.
 I don't hate you.

Hate leaves us stagnant.
I rather love or keep it pushing
We could be opposites and attract like magnets.

You being you
Doesn't stop me from being me.

We ain't crabs in a bucket
Or rats trapped in mazes that can't find the cheese.
We are human beings and sadly,

That fact still amazes as more are dead and gone.

People have short term memories
Acting like gang culture is this brand new phenomenon.
Like nomads in Germany didn't fight over territory.

It's in our natural nature to nurture hate,

Some even confuse it for glory.
Like they were born just to destroy as another man's life they take.
I don't hate you because life is too short.

We need to love more.

Damn sure doesn't mean I won't make comments
About eternal scars that leave me sore.
I just mean we should try and coexist and be equals

As citizens in a land we were born in.

Don't use excuses like border lines, races and religions to kill.
Historically, that's been human beings biggest sins. So no,
I don't hate you.

I just hate what happened to me
And hate what happened to you.

THE NEEDED CONVERSATION IN THIS WAR #144

You vs. us.
Us vs. them.

We are all human beings.
That's where the conflict begins.

Neither of us believes that
Or worse,
Neither of us know that.
Because we don't really converse,

We either tip toe

Or ignore completely.

Let's trade being uncomfortable for a little while
So that freedom reigns freely.

THE ANGEL THAT DANCED ON THE CLOUDS #145

I saw an angel today.
She danced across the clouds.
Painting all the stories
That time would allow.

The spirit resembled something
Of whimsy and lust.
I may have been high
Off substances like angel dust.

But I was in a state
Of pure sobriety.
I could see the angel's light
Shining off this energy,

Beauty
Within this entity.
And the clouds were in the shape of pianos
Playing a lovely song.

I wish she kept moving
On and on
To last forever
Or whatever time would allow.

She was the beautiful angel
That danced on the clouds.
I weirdly feel connected
Because she comes and dances whenever I need to smile.

SERENITY #146

Let me sit here
In the eye of the storm.
Praying for times
That keeps my spirit warm.
I don't feel different when I pray.
Except I can feel my spirit at peace
With almost a feeling of levitation
Away from things that are concrete.

I wanna meditate
In your essence.
Cease thoughts
That leave me stressing.
Thoughts of love.
Thoughts of hate.
Thoughts of money.
And the weight

Of pressure
Destroying my knees and ankles.
I wanna let all that turmoil go
And break these shackles
That got a hold on me.
Body, mind, spirit,
I wanna let it all go
And feel a calming release.

From head to toe.
I want my body covered
But my spirit exposed.
I don't know if prayer works
But it feels good sitting here.
I don't know if he hears me
Or even if he's there.
Out there in the sky...

I assume heaven is the divine parts of the universe
Where only the good can go.
Previously unheard questions are heard.
You finally get the answers
Once you reach there.
Maybe he hears mine
And maybe I'll get an answer.

THE KEPT DIARY PAGE #147

We had problems.
Felt like we would fight every night.
We never talked about our problems though.
We would just have sex till things got right.
Listening to slow rap music
Just to get the motion.
We were two stone cold souls
That forgot to let in emotion.
We just didn't wanna get hurt
But we were already broken.
Felt like we were lost in the world
And yet, for us, God has chosen.
But we didn't go to church
So how could we just go and assume that.
Maybe this was the devil's creation
And we just completely ignored that.
Because it felt so good to us
Just to lay here,
Until we started yelling and fighting.
If we were honest to each other,
We only stayed together out of time and fear.
I put way too much time and energy
Just to up and leave now.
But it would have been too late
If we were married with a child.
I just couldn't do that like I thought I could.
So I gave into self sabotage.
Instead of breaking things off like a man
Because morals were only a mirage.
To hurt each other, that just wasn't the plan.
But when you're running away,
Some things you just don't understand.
We were just two people
That wanted to break even some way.
And when the dust began to settle
We just lost it all anyways.
I see that now.

THE CRUMBLED UP DIARY PAGE BEFORE THE START OVER #148

You and only you
Got me out of my mental.
You crashed my heart
Like the rental.
Like you don't know
My credentials
Like damn...
Then left me all alone.
But I did it to myself
Like a shot to the dome.
I loved you so much
But we were so wrong.
I rather have blown this up
Before we become undone.
Damn.
Now we're undone.
We never talked about this,
Clearly we weren't born transparent.
We lied to everyone we ever loved,
We even lied to our parents.
Cuz feelings hurt
And I can't take no more pain.
Then somebody told me you got married...
You left me behind once again.
Damn I wish nobody told me you got married.
Life moves too fast, life moves too scary.
I'm crashing hard
And you won't even be there to catch me.
I usually tend to avoid
Feelings that are real.
I might miss the one
If I don't attempt to feel...
Again.

THE SENT DIARY PAGE #149

What a hell of a drug,
First we locked eyes and then we fell in love.
I don't know if you fell as fast or as hard as me...
I'm not even sure how you fell for a nigga like me.
But you did and we proceeded on a Hollywood Romance.
Coffee in the morning, kisses in the evening
And at night... we danced.
My heart skipped so many beats I assumed the old me died
Or at least that's what I thought when I would look into your eyes.
Old habits die hard like Bruce Willis in the movie.
We made movies-
Let's not speak on that.
We did better when we spoke less and allowed our bodies to react.
We broke our pact.
Lies became truths way before the end.
I never should have hurt my former friend,
My distant lover from another lifetime.
Ages ago, back when you were mine,
Or at least when your heart was on rental standby.
We hurt each other too often and never apologized.
Well I'm sorry on my side.
A majority of it was mine anyways.
I still played heartbreak's slave.
Look, that's not what this is about.
Just some needed precipitation inside of love's drought.
Not to say I love you, just that I did love you
So I am sorry for hurting you.
That shouldn't have happened.

LOOKING FOR WHAT I LOST OR NEVER FOUND #150

Love is foreign.
                Hate is near.

"My daddy never showed me how to love..."

Like that's something I wanna hear!

And I was her first experience at that.
So now I had to shed a tear...
Cuz I was a bad example!

We drifted away like boats at a pier,
Then we became the iceberg
That sank the Titanic.

We were in love,
We died slow, and then abruptly panicked.

Looking for comfort from others
Instead of loving each other.
Sometimes we didn't even use rubbers

Almost like we wanted to hurt each other.
I didn't want that.
But love was too foreign.

We almost got married
From feelings we were ignoring.
It wasn't right
That we went from lovers,
To enemies,
To not even knowing each other.

Still didn't delete your number from my phone...
I'm so stupid.
I guess... I... still kinda love you.

Just not like if I was shot from Cupid.
Hate to find out that you're married
But I hope you're happy.

Sad you left me all alone,
At one time treated me worse than your daddy.
Honestly I probably deserved that back then.

I just hope you're good now.
We both deserve happiness.
I just need to tear the walls down.

We ruined each other
But we did love one another.
Like when Whitney met Bobby.

A whirlwind romance that might be killing each other.
But at one time I didn't mind to die
If only I was dying with you.

But through the rubble
I had to rebuild anew.
To find happiness

With somebody else.
Just because I lost you
Doesn't mean I have to lose myself.

Even though I almost did
When I nearly fell over the edge.
Instead I found salvation

Right on that ledge.

STARING FROM THE LEDGE OF FOREVER #151

I was on the ledge,
On the edge of forever,
Staring at the flashing lights
In a city drowned with spiteful endeavors.
I saw the flaws
But searched for the beauty.
Then I looked down
And I could actually see.
I looked out into the sea of lost souls
And found you.
More than anything I thought I wanted, but everything I needed
Was right inside of you.
So I jumped off the ledge
And f
    e
      l
        l
          for you.

SONNET 999888 #152

Does a mere mortal approach a beauty
As rare as the day is long?
A beauty even Ray could see
And would inspire Stevie to write a song.
The universe did us a favor
In the creation of you.
But at times my confidence wavers
So I hide my love from the world's view.
One day I wish I could break the chains
And let my admiration reach your ears.
Your heart plus mine would be an equal gain.
I'm timid but won't be bound to fears.
If I wrote a sonnet you would be the subject.
Put my heart on this page, I just hope you love it.

I GOT THESE QUESTIONS FOR YA
#153

If life was moving too fast
Would you slow it down?

If we disagreed philosophically
Would you still be around?

If these walls crumbled tonight
Would you help provide the shelter?

If I was in dire need of an antidote
Would you provide the nectar?

If we were stranded with no umbrella
Could you stand the rain?

If we had to withstand tough times
Could you survive the pain?

If my spirit needed something new
Would you provide that for me?

If my vision was blurry
Would you deliver some sort of clarity for me?

If I told you I love you
Would you say it back?

If I said "I love you,"
Would you say it just to say it back?

If I was transparent
Would you still lie?

If I made mistakes
Would you still compare me to your ex guy?

Would you even believe me

If I told you I wasn't that guy?
Do you believe in the narrative

That all guys are the same?

And that they are only here
To drive all women insane?

Or do you believe
That some are subjected to change?

And If I said I wanted your heart
Would it really be that strange?

If I told you I love you
Would you believe that?

Do you need proof,
If so, I'll provide those facts.

Or really...
Are you just into self sabotage?

With this engraved spirit
That happiness is all a mirage?

But what if I begged you
To not let that mind state win?

Would you ever believe me
If I wanted to be your lover and your friend...

I really hope so.

WHAT I KNOW #154

Imma be honest.
I don't really know much.
But I know for a fact
You're the type of woman that would make me fall in love.

I mean I used to know why doves cry
And hearts tend to suffer.
Then we locked eyes,
I knew at that moment we needed each other.

I didn't know what love was
But I'm dying to learn with you.
I confused love as a saving grace,
Now I just want something that's true.

I never really knew much
But I know you the type to make me fall in love.
Well you're not the type... you're the prototype.
You're a chest of hidden knowledge that I crave more of.

LAID OUT ON THE TABLE #155

S.O.S I need your help,
I'm trapped here all alone.

If you saw me drowning
Would you leave me to continue on my own?

If so then let me drift
I've been cruising all my life.
If not then help me right now
I need your light.

Shine on me, shine on me
And never let it dim.

This isn't the last chance, but the best chance.
My uncle swore off love and I ain't tryna be him.

He met the one,
Treated her like the other ones,
Now he's in the very position I must avoid.

To not learn from the past is dumb.
You're disseminating these signs
To tell me what you should be to me.

I know what I should be to you.
So I hope you never tell me to leave
Cuz I wouldn't leave a good thing.

The best doesn't even compare to you.
I can't take any more false fantasies and mirages
To put my heart through.

You're scared and I'm scared but we should still give us a chance.
To be your safety net from my past actions wouldn't be safe
to conclude,

But I need you more than you need me

Because you love me just as hard as I love you.
If there are any facts you have to question,
Just know at least that one is true.

Save me from the pattern of heartbreak
That leaves me on an island all on my own.
Please don't leave me to drown here
All alone.

In the story of my past.
The places of no return.
In this love story
I hope there are more pages to turn.

I wanna see how we end up,
It could be beautiful.

Simply
Because the love is mutual.

We were placed on an equal playing field.
Not out to die on love's battle field
For the first time.

We may just thrive off something real.

THE LOVER'S PRAYER #156

I didn't believe in love
But I see it now.

It takes time to develop,
Five passes after the rebound.

I need my friend
And my lover to be the same.

I need my rock
To help keep me sane,

Not be the reason
I feel crazier.

Love is hard sometimes
But overall, it should feel easier.

We should be the safe haven
When the rest of the world is falling.

Always say, "I'm here"
Whenever we reach out calling.

I love you is not a phrase,
It's an action.

So I don't wanna hear, "I love you too,"
I wanna feel your reaction.

I WANT THIS FOREVER #157

Everlasting,
I wanna feel while deep within the spirit of the night
Where the music is played loud
And the creatures don't bite.

Well, unless you ask them to.
I live deep within the belly of the beast,
Where I may even overcome my fears.
Even though my past reveals my nature to retreat,

I may just be the mistake you regret or revel in when the sun rises.
So decide in the morning and enjoy me while it lasts.
I heard the good die young
Because good things don't last.

So just lay right here and savor every moment
Because it could all end fast.
Everlasting,
Not cuz it is,

But because after the moment that is us
Will just live
Forever...
So shouldn't we be there to enjoy it to?

I promise you I don't need perfection,
The only thing I need is you.
Lust and love can only mix perfectly
When it's done between us two.

So I need more out of forever
If forever involves you.

PRESERVED EUPHORIA #158

Two souls collide in the night sky
To produce waterfalls reigning down.
Euphoria is created because when two souls are lost,
They don't just wanna be loved, they wanna be found.
Rainbow clouds start to form.
There is beauty all around.
It's captivating,
At least that's what their eyes see.
This momentum of energy starts to surround them
As their third eyes start to meet.
Beauty from within the paradox,
The outside world is dark but inside...
It's a moment preserved for an eternity in heaven's gaze.
It's not drugs but the feeling gets them high.
It's not drugs but...
They use each other to get by.
Positively,
They lift each other up.
Memories they both shared
And will never give up.
They just want that forever kind of love.
Sometimes forever ain't enough.
I mean nothing good lasts forever,
It just feels like they could be the exception.
Rain washes the pain away
As love shields them from deception.
Time rots their bodies
But their hearts remain pure.
The outside world decays,
It was love that kept them pure.

I'M SCARED TOO #159

Look umm... I know you're scared.
I am too.
Didn't have no life instructor
Or guru.

No mentor
To help guide me on what to do.
For the most part,
I've been living wrong.
Feels like my mistakes have been going on and on
And on and on.
Like the song that was playing
When Eryka Badu met Andre 3 stacks.

So it's safe to assume that I've been heartbroken before
And can't survive another heart attack.
But I can see the light at the end of the tunnel
When I see your face.
 I've been a rolling stone half my life.
You made me wanna stand still right here in this space.
My life used to move within the speeding bullet.
You are able to slow everything down into this comfortable pace

That I can't ignore.
I've seen me transform
Into the person I should have been
Without any formal, forced uniform.
 This is me,
Like when Musiq Soulchild sings R&B.
I just wanna be the one for you
And have that be a statement we both believe.

Not even as a fact, but as feeling.
Because we are not just bodies, we are entities
That once traveled within the dark
But found its way to the light.

THE NERVOUS LOVE NOTE #160

To whom this may concern,

It's not simply the fact that my heart has this song lyric,
"All I do... is think about you," playing in constant rotation at the sight of you,
But umm... it's just that I have all this energy engulfed by love that I just wanna give
And I think I could give it to you or at least I should give it to you.
And that honestly scares the hell out of me and not the simple act of loving you,
I'd enjoy doing that for you.
No, it's just that I feel like I have no choice in the matter, like I couldn't stop it if I tried.
It's this unstoppable force like a freight train moving at the speed of light
And it's hitting me so hard that my soul can't stand
And it fell for you.
I can't ignore this... and I can't ignore you.

Signed,
Scared but ready.

SHOUTING FROM THE MOUNTAIN TOPS #161

Your voice is a beautiful melody.
Our bodies create a beautiful harmony.
It's you who I wanna see when I go to sleep
Whether short term or eternally.

Compliments to the most high, he did a
Good job when creating thee.
Face forever engraved in my memory.
Engraved in stone and your love is the carver's tool.
I hope your heart remains overflowing instead of merely full.
You have so much love to give
With a soul that has so much life to live.
With you, I will always trip.
Emotions fall from my lips

To yours.
I truly implore
You never change.
Life without you would be strange.

That's not life but a whole new definition.
That's not life. I would be breathing, but not living.
Alive but my heart wouldn't be beating.
The sun and you are always competing.

It's your light that shines brightest.
Without you my soul would riot.
You're the coal that gets the engine in my heart reignited.
How I feel about you is too strong girl so I can't keep quiet!

MEDS NUMB THE PAIN #162

I don't know where I am
I just know you're close to where I'm at.
Ran in the sun,
Rolled in the grass.
I looked deeper,
It was actually glass.
I was cut and bleeding
But I felt nothing.
I stared at my arms
And thought it was something.
I just kept bleeding,
Life kept going.
Like if all my jackets were destroyed
And it was snowing.
As if there was no roof
While it was raining.
Or if Adam and Eve stayed ignorantly blissful
And there was no shaming.
We were just naked
Under the stars,
You and I.
Unaffected as we are.
As our heart rates slowed down...
I could feel the vibes.
Thought I had a heart attack or stroke
But then realized
It was just a pure substance with no anecdote.
Where pain leaves
And spirits grow.
You kiss me,
I remain numb from head to toe.
I don't feel a thing,
Don't need to know where to find a hospital.
It's all perfect.
Just lay right there.
In chaos, I'm ok
Cuz you're right here.

PERFECT KILLS AND THE REAL FEEDS #163

I don't want a white picket fence,
I want you.

I don't need a sunny day,
You light up my view.

I don't need new love songs,
You're a classic with a soul feel.

I don't need no vices
When you provide that addictive, sex appeal.

At first it was wrong
But it always felt right.

Life is less complicated
When you're by my side at night.

We are perfectly imperfect.
That might be what we need.

Perfection destroys
While the real feeds.

I've never been more full
Just from the appetizing blemishes between me and you.

So trust when I say I don't want perfection
Because I love every single flaw that belongs to you.

LAID UP #164

I can barely see the light
Peeking through the window.
You leave me feeling
How I do when I hit the Indo.
High.
In the metaphysical sense.
All my pain is washed away
While my conscience is rinsed.
You make me feel like dancing
Still, I'd rather lay down with you.
 Your heartbeat plays my favorite song
When it's pressed up against me and puts me in the mood.
I wanna tear your clothes off
And spread your legs
Into a peace sign.
Why make war when we can make love instead
And then lay down here for a day or two.
Lets hideaway
And leave the rest of the world
In disarray.
This bed under this roof
Is our secret hiding place.
Ducked off
Nobody should find us
Nor
Try and reach us.
Just leave us
In bliss.
Fault us
If there's anything we miss.
We'll take the loss
If you think we messed up.
But we honestly don't care what y'all have to offer.
We rather just be right here laid up.

THE VIBE #165

In the back of this lac.
Smoke clouds fog up the window.
Feet all up on my system.
I'm high off you and this indo.
This world don't even matter.
I steady travel your eyes.
Floated inside your troubled waters
And met your soul inside.

SO THANKFUL #166

Simply,
You're the greatest thing black people created since Jazz.
I wanna thank your momma
And I wanna thank your dad.

It goes beyond simple things
Like you're the best sex I ever had.
This is because when I fell for you,
I knew where I could safely land.

APOLOGIES LOVE #167

Sorry if I stare,
I was taught to appreciate art
And that's all I see in front of me.
Worth way more than a thousand words,
Love, you're priceless.

TRANSPARENT FOR THE FIRST TIME #168

My spirit is placed upon your lips
As your heart is immersed in my soul.
The taste of you is forever engraved in my memory banks.
Every moment alone with you is legendary.
I don't just mean when it's nobody else around,
I just mean that when it comes to us, nobody else really matters.
I look at you and I see a mirror,
A passage way to a better me.
There is nobody better than you.
I believe that in my heart.
Edged that fact within the walls of my spirit for all to see.

YOUR KISS #169

Your kiss ignited the fire that burned the walls down.
Made form concrete it burned like timber,
We celebrated as the walls came down.
We danced in the moonlight,
Then we made love till the sunrise.
Your kiss set two souls ablaze,
Melting them into one vibrant heart beat.
One wavelength that never wanted to be estranged again,
You had me searching this earth alone all these years,
I'm just glad we found each other.
Now I have clarity
In this flawed world we reside in.
Rihanna told us to find love in a hopeless place.
Well your kiss gave my world hope
As the walls were set ablaze.

GHETTO ASS LOVE #170

I can be your nigga.
You can be my bitch.
That's only for us,
The outside world doesn't exist.
We can't suffocate
Through bills
While avoiding
These cheap thrills.
Cuz love is an obstacle course
That we're just trynna live in.
We'll pray for forgiveness,
Cuz honestly, we'll probably still sin.
I hope you can accept me,
I love your flaws too.
Get your fucking ass on that bed
Cuz you love it when I'm a tad bit rude.
But if anyone else disrespects
That's a 9 feet dirt nap for that dude.
6 feet is required
But those extra three are for you.
Passion runs our spirits,
Emotions control our actions,
The brain will always lose
When it's the heart that wants a reaction.
So Imma grab you in close
And Imma hold you real tight.
Love is a war and this is our battlefield
So Imma lay you down tonight.
That ghetto love affair,
So when I say you're mine, you're mine.
I can warm up your heart
Then make you arch your spine.
We're living something real.
Addictive,
Not just because of your sex appeal,
You fed me words
That heal.

I want you day and night
Like a Kid Cudi song
And lately I have different uses
For classic sad songs.
I enjoy the art
Instead of having them cleanse my wrongs.
I love it.
I love you.
Love used to hurt
And sent me to my doom.
Until I fell for you,
Now we are the only ones in any room.
The outside world doesn't matter…
It doesn't even exist
Because I've been madly in love with you
From our first kiss.
Now I need you like the air I breathe
That fills my lungs.
Before you, the phrase "I love you,"
Never meant a thing when it left my tongue.
You give love a face.
A brand new meaning.
You breathed life into the word forever,
Transforming it into a feeling.

A RATCHET ROMANTIC #171

Sex on the beach while we listen to Jodeci.
I brought you flowers, candy and bottles of Hennessy
To enjoy while we smoke this weed and talk about life
upon this balcony.
We look upon the stars and see the stories they tell...
Then go inside and get these rounds girl I ain't ringing no bell.
You my piece of heaven when I'm going through hell
So Imma lay your body down like a man that's preparing for jail.
Red roses and green leaves make up your bouquet.
I wanna kiss you, while you're sitting on the bathroom sink,
listening to Sade.
I wanna take this ice cube and rub it slow against your body....
Only because you got excited about that when we watched *Do the Right Thing*,
But if we watching *Love & Basketball*, then we on our Maxwell thing.
This Woman's Work is the soundtrack while you got your
t-shirt and panties on.
Whenever you're my private dancer girl that really turns me on.
You even bought a stripper pole, you dope for that.
Addictive in the purest form like if coke was back.
If you kiss me then I'll kiss you back...
You're probably the reason why Digital Underground
had to write that.
Seduction from your lips,
First we French inhale then we French kiss.
We may two step, then slow dance, and I'll work in a little dip.
You by yourself are enough motivation.
I felt nothing till you provided the sensation.
You are a beautiful creation
And me kissing you is like a celebration
To what your parents made.
At first I just wanted to get laid
But now I feel like it's a home we made...
And it's beautiful inside...
A place made for two for the one that's down to ride
With rose petals, 40 ounces and blunts lit by candle light.

My soul was in the dark but you helped me reach the light.
I appreciate you for that always.

THE DREAM #172

I want a love so fierce
They teach you about it in a poetry class.
Like this style was created to help the passion burn brightest
So their love would last.

I wanna live forever
Like them Shakespeare characters
Printed in bold in them history books
So I know you heard of us.

I'm happy with you
To be whatever God has aligned.
Just to be frozen in gold
Within the hands of time.

I want it all as long as you're mine,
I say this with all honesty.
Not a prize, you're priceless,
But you're so dear to me.

I fell for your body
But fell in love with your spiritual energy.
I want a love that's engulfing
Like the tornado that Dorothy was swept in

To take me to places I've never seen before
Like the Land of Oz where everything can begin.
I seen hope reside
Within your eyes.

It draws me in with covert power,
That's where my devotion lies.
I want a love so amazing
It all feels like a dream.

I want a love like the one we got right now in this moment
So I pray to God that I never wake up from this dream.
Fantasies excite my spirit when I lay down
And go to sleep
And wake up
Just to find you still laying next to me.
Yeah that's the dream.
I love this Dream.

THE SWITCH UP #173

Love is simple.
Hate is hard.
Love is kind.
Hate is harsh.
Love is right here.
Hate is broad.
Love is clearly specific.
Hate is so abstract.

I could hate it all
And still want you attached.
I could hate all the days to come-
Still smile anytime you come around.

Stress just seems less prevalent
When you're around.

Love is simple.
Hate is hard.

Love helps the soul,
Mends the heart.
Hate deteriorates the soul,
Poisons thoughts.
I rather be in love with you
Than continue to hate me.

You made it so I could come out of the darkness
And find a better me.

YOU #174

I see the art in your bare curves.
You shine in the moonlight, the spotlight you deserve.
The melanin on your skin is this overwhelming, graceful presence.
Pure beauty within its essence.
It looks like gold and taste like my favorite cake.
I love your shape.
I love your eyes; I can see eternity inside them.
Happiness resides from inside them
And exudes an engulfing flame from without.
Sometimes I wanna shout
I love your eyes!
There's this addiction I have with your hips and thighs.
Besides your lips and eyes, they're the first things I see.
Whether a sundress, skin tight clothes or jeans.
You're a sculpture and anywhere you go turns into an art museum.
Eyes follow you anywhere you go; they are slaves to your every whim.
You still carry yourself with this undeserved humility
Like you don't know how amazing you are, really?
I'm in awe of you.

WHAT I WANNA DO #175

I wanna be the ship that cruises in the night,
Crashing into your ocean.
I was a dog in my past life,
That's why you have all my devotion.
I wanna be the straw that stirs your tea,
So slow...
Then speed it up
As long as you never let it go.
I want your lips tattooed on my neck.
No mistakes.
No regrets.
It's just proof
That you're the touch I can't forget.
The touch that I still reminisce
During my daydreams.
Your sex is fantasies
Mixed with wet dreams
That would be in romance novels
That couldn't be read by preteens.
There's an age limit to this
And we meet that.
I see your body sway when you walk
And I need that.
I'll tell you again
Baby I need that!
I see your body sway nude in the moonlight
And I crave that!
That was just a little extra herbs and spices
For this full course meal.
I hope that this sticks to your ribs
While providing something real.
I wanna be like steak,
Except healthy for ya.
I prefer you naked, that's body and soul,
Just know I adore ya.
So I'll do what I'm supposed to.
Stir up emotions you'll be happy I evoked.

I can hear your body talking to me
And this is what it spoke
"Dive into this love.
Dive into this passion.
No games played.
Only about this action."
Hope you feel every word
Cuz I'm not into no acting.
Just wanna kiss your forehead, place you on this bed,
And make the kind of love that feels everlasting.

SOMETHING I WROTE FOR YOU #176

My mind goes from PG to Rated-R when I see you.
I don't have to hit it but Imma at least try whenever I'm around you.
Face to face... chest to chest... I love that point of view.
I just need your body in the worst way and don't care if that ever comes off rude.
It's not just physical because it's spiritual too.
Two souls that fit together perfectly without being super glued,
Meaning we aren't just forcing something that
We're not supposed to.
We're just allowing fate to guide us towards the heaven that was made for us two.
You tease me a lot and I kinda like it too.
I stare at your frame so you do a little dance when it's just us two.
Just to let me know that you know where my eyes are going to.
They gonna stay there for a while boo.
I like kissing, holding, dancing, talking and just looking at you.
Love any action that leads to you moaning ooooo.
Sorry, I went PG to Rated-R again like that's something
I can choose.
You bring my brain to mush at the single thought of you.
Yet clarity was present when I told you,
"I Love You."
I don't believe the person you love is something you can choose
But each and every time I'd always choose you.

WHAT I ALWAYS NEEDED #177

Your thick thighs are my playground
With those pretty brown eyes I could bathe in.

Your touch is my safe haven.
My lips match up like puzzle pieces to your sun soaked skin.

Beauty queen with shy girl tendencies.
Walking around like you don't know your own identity.

When the world crumbles around me
You'll still be my serenity.

Lips taste like heaven dipped in sugar.
Hips move like a snake, I'm hypnotized in your figure.

You're what I want and what I need.
When you talk that talk my spirit quivers.

I love this.
I love you.

Spirit dipped in perfection,
Yet God put me in front of you?

I don't deserve you but I won't question his decision.
I'll just cherish you.

Make you smile everyday
With a couple of nice words to say.

A woman like you
Don't deserve no more rainy days.

No M.D. in our names,
But we performed surgery on our open hearts

To mend ourselves from past pains

And wash away all the marks and scars
That was left behind.

I walked this Earth alone for many years
And it was you that filled that void.

I could feel our love build
Instead of letting pain destroy.

I'm thankful for that.

I JUST WANNA LOVE YOU #178

I know you're broken baby,
I am too.

But if you want to pick up the pieces,
I'll be your superglue.

I asked, "Who are you?"
And you revealed yourself.

So I took my broken, battered heart
Right up off that shelf.

I displayed it to you, meekly,
But still my prized possession.

It was left out in the storm
Without any form of hesitation.

But you held it
Like it was this rare entity to behold.

So I want to love you
Well beyond the time our bodies grow old

Inside this love story
The universe has told.

I just wanna love you!
I just wanna love you.

I PRAYED TO GOD ABOUT YOU
#179

I prayed to God about you.
I prayed to God I'd meet you.
I wasn't sure on religion
But I'm so sure about you.

I needed a higher power.
I needed a resolution.
I am a broken man.
You found a new solution.

I am on bended knee-
Because I cannot stand.
I lost all my strength,
I don't feel like a man.

I seen you in my dreams,
I feel like you're what God has planned.
We don't talk too often.
This time I tried to listen and understand.

I can't say you equal
All my unanswered questions.
I just think that I love you
And that we were destined.

I prayed to God about you.
I prayed to God I'd meet you.
I wasn't sure on religion
But I'm so sure about you.

VI.

UNTITLED SPIRIT #180

Love has the spirit to create and kill
Not even at free will, that's how strong its spirit is
Hate is just love that was misplaced or overflowing
To love and to hate is to care without reason or wit
One just does it
Some kill and some die,
Some try to react and some try to survive
But one just does
Because love just does
Something that is
Or never was...

CLARITY FROM WITHIN THE ASHES OF THE MIDNIGHT HOUR
is....

A collection of poems constructed together to tell the story of a young black male that was struggling to find happiness within a chaotic environment. He clings on to this relationship that he believes is love but was principally made from lust. Constantly being presented with images of people that look like him die to no consequence, he begins to acknowledge what he believes society is trying to tell him. The pursuit of happiness wasn't written down for you. Yet his toughest task may be trying to cope with his own thoughts while everything is quiet and he is all alone. A way to cope and keep moving is all he asks for. Black people are not taught to express and heal. They are taught to repress and survive: a coping mechanism that was developed in the days of slavery. He wants love, but at times, struggles to find ways to even love himself.

RASHAD KHYRE KENNEDY
is...

A singer, songwriter from Long Beach, California who goes by the stage name of P. Charms. Rashad is also a writer of poetry and stories. He found his love of poetry and storytelling from school and rap music. Predominantly, Tupac Shakur's music and poetry inspired him to write his thoughts down. Tupac made learning and writing poetry interesting to Rashad while the other kids treated it as cruel and unusual punishment. Most importantly, Rashad is a young black man that is attempting to find his place in a world that doesn't seem to love him, such as the character in the book. The words on the pages felt freeing at a time where the author felt suffocated. To him, writing these words out was cheaper than therapy. He hopes you are able to gain something from the works of poetry: whether that is happy, sad, anger, inspiration, enjoyment or closure.

If YOU ENJOYED THE BOOK AND WANT TO HEAR MORE, CONTACT ME HERE:

Email: rkk8008@yahoo.com
Instagram: @pcharmsfkmusic
Facebook: Rashad Pcharms Kennedy
Website: www.pcharmsfkmusic.com

www.ingramcontent.com/pod-product-compliance
Lightning Source LLC
Chambersburg PA
CBHW041611220426
43668CB00004B/44